Solution-Focused Pastoral Counseling

Solution-Focused Pastoral Counseling

An Effective Short-Term Approach for Getting People Back on Track

Charles Allen Kollar

GRAND RAPIDS, MICHIGAN 49530

ZONDERVAN™

Solution-Focused Pastoral Counseling

Requests for information should be addressed to:

Zondervan, *Grand Rapids, Michigan 49530*

Library of Congress Cataloging-in-Publication Data

Kollar, Charles Allen, 1953–
Solution-focused pastoral counseling : an effective short-term approach for getting people back on track / Charles Allen Kollar.
p. cm.
Includes bibliographical references and index.
ISBN 0-310-21346-0 (alk. paper)
1. Pastoral counseling. 2. Solution-focused therapy—Religious aspects—Christianity. 3. Short-term counseling—Religious aspects—Christianity. I. Title.
BV4012.2.K67 1997
253'.5—dc21 96-51062

This edition is printed on acid-free paper.

Interior design by Sue Vandenberg Koppenol

Printed in the United States of America

02 03 04 05 06 07 /❖ DC/ 14 13 12 11 10 9 8 7

Contents

Preface

The intended audiences for this book are primarily pastors, counselors within the local church, and students preparing for pastoral ministry. Although the book presents a single theoretical approach to counseling, it is not intended to reduce counseling approaches to this one option. Rather, it presents a natural and spontaneous view of Christian maturation and gives a specific procedure for encouraging that growth from within the counseling process. The primary counselor is always the Holy Spirit. If this approach encourages the reader regarding the counseling portion of his ministry, it has served its purpose.

Certain explanations are in order at this point: (1) In most cases throughout this book the masculine pronoun is used in a generic and inclusive fashion. This is intended to make writing and, I hope, reading easier. (2) Scripture quotations are from the *New International Version* unless otherwise noted. All use of Scripture is for illustrative purposes only and is not intended to impute biblical authority to any portion of this theoretical approach. (3) The titles *pastor, minister, elder, Christian leader,* and *church counselor* are used interchangeably. (4) Today the term *pastoral counselor* often refers to one who counsels professionally for a fee. The American Association of Pastoral Counselors (AAPC) certifies counselors, offering clear academic, professional, and ethical guidelines. Therefore, when speaking of those who counsel within the local church, I often use the expression *church counselors*. This in no way implies lesser ability or competence. Church counselors often have excellent credentials, but they rarely receive pay for counseling services. (5) I believe that the use of the term *counselee* is preferable to *client*, which implies that the counselor receives pay, and *patient*, which implies physical illness or disease. Although sometimes confusing to the eye, the terms *counselor* and *counselee* appear together often throughout this book. (6) The term *interview* is used when referring to the first counseling appointment; second or subsequent appointments are referred to as *sessions*.

(7) The identities of counselees in the case studies of this book have been carefully disguised in accordance with professional standards of confidentiality and in keeping with the rights of counselees to privileged communication with the author. All names and identifying background information have been changed. (8) *All case studies* represent portions of counseling sessions and relationships. They are presented in various forms throughout the text to illustrate the immediate context. They are not offered to imply that major problems can be solved simply, nor that they can always be solved in two or three sessions. They are intended only to illustrate that counselees can make the required *shift in thinking* in that amount of time and can get refocused regarding the solutions to their problems. Future sessions are often spaced further apart in order to facilitate the counselee's personal observations of being on track.

Introduction

This book is written for pastors and other Christian leaders who counsel, or wish to counsel, within the local church. Many have expressed a desire to offer counseling that is effective and short-term. They are seeking an affirming and positive way to help their congregations. Solution-Focused Pastoral Counseling (SFPC) offers an alternative to all problem-focused counseling approaches, whether they come from the Bible or from secular counseling models. Its intention is to provide counselors with the how-to's for staying on track during the counseling interview—as well as helping individuals, couples, or families get unstuck and back on track.

The material is presented in two parts. Part 1, chapters 1–8, explains and illustrates the *theoretical model* that supports this approach. Chapter 1 discusses our personal paradigms and how they can blind us to other options. Chapter 2 considers the struggle between expecting the power of God to change lives quickly and recognizing the need for Christians to seek counseling—often from professional therapists.

Chapter 3 presents an overview of the world of mental health and introduces the concept of deficiency language. Chapter 4 explores the hidden presuppositions that all counselors reveal by their use of questions within the counseling setting. It reveals what these presuppositions are and how they direct the conversation, sometimes without our knowing it.

Chapter 5 addresses the issue of personal constructs, i.e., the constant process all of us are engaged in as we seek to make sense of what we experience in life. Chapter 6 explains how God's grace affects our personal constructs, endowing them with new meaning and forming our individual identities. Chapter 7 submits the nine guiding assumptions that inform this solution-focused approach. Chapter 8 presents some ethical guidelines that should guide the practice of counseling.

Part 2, chapters 9–16, moves us from theory to *practice*. Chapter 9 introduces a flowchart that depicts a conceptual schema for SFPC. Its intent is to serve as a map showing various avenues for creating outcome-focused conversations. Chapters 10 through 13 develop and illustrate the four processes of SFPC, demonstrating a framework for change.

Chapter 14 gives guidance for consolidating change if second or subsequent sessions are needed. Chapter 15 offers a case illustration that brings the entire SFPC approach together. Finally, chapter 16 offers a few final thoughts in response to questions I have been asked regarding this approach.

Acknowledgments

Many thanks to my friends and colleagues who reviewed this manuscript for me, offering numerous valuable suggestions and encouragement: Judy Balswick, professor at Fuller Theological Seminary; Del Tarr, president, Assemblies of God Theological Seminary; Peggy Ebinger, psychiatrist at Avery Finney Associates; Richard Fox, director of Shepherd Staff Counseling Center; Paul Van Valin, director of Eden Counseling Center; Bill Butler, counselor at Psychotherapy Services of Ghent; Jerry Qualls, senior pastor at Glad Tidings Church, Norfolk, Virginia; Ronald Traub and Gene Nelson, professors at Valley Forge Christian College; Stan Gundry and Ed van der Maas at Zondervan for believing in this work; and Jim Ruark for his supportive editing.

Special thanks to my brother Frank—without whose initial urging and envisioning this project would never have gotten off the ground; and to my parents—Mom, whose imagination took root within all her children, and Dad, whose perseverance and leadership paved the way.

Finally, to my children—Nathan, Joshua, and Heather—who offer an endless supply of illustrative material and for whom I thank God each day; and to my wife, Dawn—my lover, partner, and best friend for the past twenty years—who read and reread my initial manuscript and whose support is constant. The truest person I know.

PART ONE

Theory

CHAPTER ONE

Individual Paradigms: A Question of Focus

The mind is a lot like an umbrella—it works best when it is open. ■ *Anonymous*

If we do not change our direction, we are likely to end up where we are headed. ■ *Ancient Chinese Proverb*

Nothing is more dangerous than an idea when it is the only one you have. ■ *Emile Chartier*

I have often wondered what it is that prevents us from seeing and acting on new ideas. It is important to understand this because it is probably the same thing that hinders a counselee from seeing new options, possibilities, and solutions. Something blinds our vision when we are in the midst of a crisis or problem-saturated life situation. We assume that the future is only an extension of the past. Yet when it comes to problems, one assumption is clear: If you keep doing what you have always been doing, you will keep getting what you have always been getting.

We all have self-imposed rules and regulations that establish our personal boundaries. We learn how to be successful within these boundaries. These perimeters are our *individual paradigms*. They filter all incoming information, filtering out whatever does not fit. Jesus commented on humanity's inability to see beyond its paradigms when He taught about the kingdom of God. What He said was unlike anything His listeners had ever heard before. It did not fit their rules and regulations. To many of them it was as if they were entirely deaf. Of such Jesus said, "If anyone has ears to hear, let him hear" (Mark 4:23).

Because of our fixed paradigms we often miss out on discovering future possibilities. Unexpected information is ignored or twisted to fit old notions. Sometimes it seems invisible. *We are blind to creative solutions.* Our paradigms have the power to keep us from hearing and seeing what could happen. This results in personal limitations, a kind of intellectual myopia.

My son Nathan recently did a school report on Galileo. I think I learned as much as he did through his presentation. I was reminded of the religious and civic leaders that Galileo had to contend with. They were unable to see or hear his observations regarding the earth's orbiting the sun. These observations simply did not fit their personal paradigms. Everyone "knew" that the sun revolved around the earth! Although seeing, they did not see. Hearing, they did not hear. Of course history has revealed their shortsightedness. We would never be as blind and deaf as they, or would we? We would, and we often are—usually without knowing it.

Consider the devastating lesson the Swiss watch manufacturers learned. Just thirty years ago Swiss watches were the standard of excellence throughout the world. Nearly 80 percent of all watches sold were made by Swiss watchmakers. Today fewer then 10 percent are made by the Swiss. Thousands of expert craftsmen lost their jobs. How did this happen?

In one sense they were blinded by the incredible achievement and all the successes of their old paradigm. Even a prosperous past can blind us to future possibilities. It was a Swiss technician who created the quartz watch. He had managed to reach beyond the paradigm that watches *must* have gears and springs. His superiors, however, still blinded by their paradigm, declared, "Who ever heard of such a thing! Watches must have gears and springs!" They were so sure of their convictions that they did not bother to protect their ownership of the technician's design. Some years later the quartz watch was displayed at a world's fair. Representatives from two young companies were very much interested in it. One representative was from Seiko and the other from Texas Instruments. The rest is history.

As counselors within the local church, have we fallen into a similar trap regarding counseling? It must be done a certain way or it just is not counseling. One thing we are all convinced of is that we need to understand and deal with the problem. It has been said that to define a problem is to begin to solve it. We must explore the problem and perhaps discover how the counselee is thinking, feeling, or behaving. There must be a reason. Why is it happening? What is maintaining it?

Whether the counselor uses psychological theories and methods or the approach of admonishing from the authority of Scripture, either way the paradigm is centered squarely on the problem. This is what I call a *problem-focused paradigm*. This is the very reason the counselee has come for counseling. He is so focused on his problem that it is affecting him negatively. So what do we do as counselors? We usually focus squarely on the problem! We are going to help him get to the root of his problem no matter how hard it is or how long it takes! Is there a better way? Perhaps it just takes a little imagination to discover a better way.

For years Disney cartoonists have used a concept called *imagineering* to assist them in creating their wonderful movies. They carefully visualize their outcome, a perfect cartoon. We could view this as a "problem-free" cartoon. When the artist is creating this perfect cartoon, what will he be doing first? What next? and so on, one frame at a time. Imagineering is a paradigm buster. When we visualize the outcome first, we become *solution-focused* rather than problem-focused. *The outcome dictates the process, rather than the process dictating the outcome.*

This book is about "imagineering" with those who come to us for counseling. It is about clear procedures for getting them unstuck and back on track in their lives, marriages, and families. It is about busting paradigms regarding how counseling is done—both in the mind of the counselor and of the counselee.

It is my belief that counseling should be fun and spontaneous. The traditional paradigm that counseling must primarily focus on the problem is an unhelpful idea that has hindered counselors for years. My hope is that this book will encourage the reader to see beyond a problem-focused paradigm, while providing helpful guidelines and skills for creative goal formation in the counseling interview. ■

CHAPTER TWO

Christian Faith: A Story of Change

Therefore, if anyone is in Christ, he is a new creation; the old has gone, the new has come! ▪ *2 Corinthians 5:17*

I've learned that the most creative ideas come from beginners—not the experts. ▪ *H. Jackson Brown, Jr., 1991, p. 99*

The apostle Paul announces a totally unanticipated new beginning. What he describes in his letter to the church at Corinth reflects a profound change. In Christ, the believer's personal control is being reestablished and hope has been restored. All this happens in spite of the problems the new believer is facing. Often the solution that Paul offers does not seem to have any direct connection to the problem at all. The solution amounts to an entirely new way of perceiving life—an extraordinary shift of paradigms.

As both a pastor and a professional counselor, I have discovered a struggle between knowing that the power of God can change lives quickly and recognizing the need for Christians to seek counseling. This dichotomy exists throughout this book. It is intentional and, I believe, unavoidable. It represents the internal contradictions that exist side by side within my own philosophy of ministry. On the one hand, as a pastor

I have come to depend on *and assume* the presence of the creative activity of the Spirit of God. Thus my understanding of counseling also assumes this creative activity. New life in Christ needs to be prompted and encouraged. A solution-focused approach to pastoral counseling specifically seeks to move the counselee *forward* into his new life.

On the other hand, during the past ten years I have, as a counselor, also entered the *world of mental health.* This is the designation I use to describe a system that seems to maintain its own hierarchy and tenets of faith. This world focuses on the small percentage of our population who are afflicted with a physical dysfunction of the brain, resulting in a mental disorder. But many well-intentioned practitioners overgeneralize, applying this same concept of mental disease to the mass of people who struggle with emotional problems. The church must not succumb to this same overgeneralization.

As I perceive it, at the top of the hierarchy are the psychiatrists—medical doctors who are highly skilled psychopharmacologists. Their priority is the utilization of psychotropic or mind-altering medications. Next are the clinical psychologists who, having their doctorates in psychology, are experts within this field. Then come the therapists, who are licensed and highly trained academically—at least at a graduate level, and often at a doctoral level as well. All of these professionals may represent dozens of therapeutic approaches. Some are eclectic, and others may focus more on social services. Finally, underlying this hierarchy is the pharmaceutical industry, which has millions of dollars invested in the world of mental health.

Here is where the division lies within my own philosophy of ministry today. The pastoral side is crying out, "Slow down!" Are we, like Esau, selling our inheritance for a bowl of stew? Why do I ask this? Because pastors are not represented anywhere within the hierarchy of the world of mental health. We are often relegated to a subordinate position beneath therapists, useful as referral agents. Religion is often dismissed to the domain of personal faith alone. The hierarchy within the mental health system has the stamp of scientific approval upon it, so the pastor should not venture into an arena where he is not qualified to minister. Yet the *therapist* side of me has seen individuals so overwhelmed by mental confusion that most pastors *would* be out of their depth in knowing what to do—*especially* when in dealing with such persons they try to make use of the small amount of psychological training they may have had.

I believe the church must maintain a friendly working relationship with the world of mental health. Yet we must reject any implied notion of *subordination*, or we are at risk of placing the power and grace of God into a subordinate role as well. We must take back the role of counseling within the local church. If not, there is another "world" ready to take leadership in this field. If we *are* to refer a counselee into that world, then let us refer him to Christians who are aware of the capabilities of the Spirit of God within the counselee and the recognized limitations of psychological theory. Christian counselors who choose to function professionally within the world of mental health also believe in new life through Christ. Many of my colleagues consider their calling within the mental health community a ministry, and they have dedicated their time and efforts to it. Many recent books on mental health published for the church have been written by those who minister in this fashion.

SUBORDINATION

It seems to me, however, that pastors often see *themselves* as capable only of assisting a person with salvation and engaging him in training and discipleship. After all, serious problems must be entrusted to an expert. How have we become convinced of this?

Most pastors have had a few courses in psychology and sociology, and these have opened to them a whole new perspective on human development. But in each course the message has come through loud and clear: this is a discipline that you must become expert in if you expect to utilize it successfully. And of course in a sense this is true. If you simply meddle in psychology, you can do more harm than good. Most ministers realize that they are far from expert in this field. Usually the few courses we take on counseling are very practical in nature, e.g., how to counsel parishioners with minor problems and when to refer them to expert counseling. Indeed, we are told that the best thing we can do for a counselee is to know how to refer and to whom to refer.

Some Christian writers today imply that the pastor is subordinate to professional counselors. He is unequipped to effectively counsel anyone who has a serious mental disorder. Christian psychologists continue to publish books that reinforce this basic belief, even as they try to help the pastor counsel more effectively in regard to the basic problems people face.

Of course it is true that a pastor is an inadequate counselor—if he *must* be an expert on emotional problems to be effective. But must a counselor be an expert? The apostle Paul wrote that God is already at work in the counselee (2 Cor. 4:12; 1 Thess. 2:13). He is a letter from Christ, written with the Spirit of the living God, not on a tablet of stone but on a tablet of a human heart (2 Cor. 3:3). I believe the counselor's task is to look for this *writing of the Spirit* in the counselee's life, rather than concentrating on present or past problems. This is what ministers *are* expert at doing.

MENTAL HEALTH

Paul wrote to another church, "I have become [a] servant by the commission God gave me to present to you the word of God in its fullness. . . . We proclaim him, admonishing and teaching everyone with all wisdom, so that we may present everyone perfect in Christ" (Col. 1:25, 28). This perfection is not positional, but actual. The word "perfect" here refers to being complete in all that pertains to personal growth, mental health, and moral character. It is the life of God in the counselee, placed there by the Word and the Spirit, that is making the Christian "perfect."

One Christian author who is a successful psychologist wrote, "Churches have a woefully simplistic understanding of the problems people experience. A fair number seem to glory in their ignorance by insisting there is no need for an inside look" (Crabb, 1991, p. 51). I know what he means, and it does happen. But how can ministers and other church leaders who counsel be effective when the standard for competence regarding emotional illness originates from the discipline of psychology?

When a minister reads a book on counseling, he often feels like a fish out of water. How is he going to find the time to use these theories properly? Many feel the frustration of having little to build on because their foundation for teaching and training is through faith, Scripture, and the church. A pastor's strength is the Word of God and an understanding of the sanctifying work of the Holy Spirit, not psychological theory.

I have wondered if pastors, through the educational process, have come to believe that their pastoral training is inferior to psychological training? Again, ministers are not considered real players within the hierarchy of the mental health community. Many have experienced a tragic loss of confidence in their authority and ability to counsel. This loss of confidence has often been reinforced by some psychiatric centers whose marketing strategy is to convince ministers and other Christian leaders to send their parishioners to them for professional psychological help.

However, through personal experience and through relationships with other professional counselors, I have discovered that psychological methods and therapeutic approaches are not always very effective. Often they are not much more than guesswork and sometimes actually reinforce the client's problems. The primary diagnostic tool of the professional counseling community, the *Diagnostic and Statistical Manual*, now in its fourth edition (American Psychiatric Association, 1994), is used for the diagnosis of mental disorders. But more than that, *it gives structure to an entire way of perceiving reality.* It is offered as a guideline for understanding a counselee.

TRUTH

As a Christian it was my encounter with Jesus, my belief that he was speaking the truth and was totally worthy of my trust, that transformed my life. It was this same truth that altered my perception of reality. And it was this altered perception that gave me the ability to see through difficult problems and take hold of solutions as actualities already accomplished. Some professional therapists now use forms of counseling that focus on solutions, spurning many of the psychological beliefs of the past seventy years. It is interesting that, after years of skepticism, the Christian community is embracing the very beliefs these secular therapists are calling into question.

These therapists are returning to a common-sense approach to counseling that is suspicious of all diagnostic labels or mental-disorder classifications. Their intent now is to focus on the positive strengths of their clients rather than on their weaknesses and problems. I deeply appreciate my training as a professional counselor, but some of it created within me a problem-focused paradigm.

AGREEMENT WITH GOD'S INTENTION

The prophet Amos wrote, "Do two walk together unless they have agreed to do so?" (Amos 3:3). The counselor and the counselee must be in agreement with *God's intention* if the counselee is to make any progress. In going to a professional counselor, a parishioner is often removed from many of his primary sources of strength: a caring and loving church counselor; a healthy and supportive community of fellow believers; and, most important, the transforming power of the Word of God. Some counselors believe that it is helpful to remove the parishioner from the church setting. I disagree with this in light of the scriptural insistence that the believer is to grow *within* the community of the local church, where there is accountability to others and for others, along with acceptance. Paul implied as much when he wrote,

"Speaking the truth in love, we will in all things grow up into him who is the Head, that is, Christ" (Eph. 4:15).

Although Scripture has a great deal to say about looking within, at our hearts, it does so from the perspective of remorse, forgiveness, cleansing, and discernment. As the apostle Paul wrote, "Brothers, I do not consider myself yet to have taken hold of it. But one thing I do: Forgetting what is behind and straining toward what is ahead, I press on toward the goal to win the prize for which God has called me heavenward in Christ Jesus" (Phil. 3:13–14).

Paul encourages the Christian to press forward toward God's unfolding purpose, trusting God each step of the way. In the same passage he also instructs us to "live up to" what we have already attained. *This assumes that God has already placed into our lives much of what He considers necessary for us to begin making progress regarding our spiritual and emotional growth.*

So what alternative is there to becoming an expert in psychology? An effective alternative is to train ministers and leaders in the local church to counsel at a professional level, through that which God in His wisdom has already supplied—the strengths of the counselee. That is what this book is all about. ■

CHAPTER THREE

Deficiency Language: The World of Mental Health

Keep clear of psychiatrists unless you know that they are also Christians. Otherwise they start with the assumption that your religion is an illusion and try to "cure" it: and this assumption they make not as professional psychologists but as amateur philosophers. ▪ *C. S. Lewis, 1966*

Of all the tyrannies a tyranny sincerely exercised for the good of its victims may be the most oppressive. ▪ *C. S. Lewis, 1970*

WILLIAM'S STORY

William Johnson nearly died in a terrorist attack ten years ago in Israel. The pointless bloodshed and loss of life haunt him to this day. He had been a moderate drinker for years before this senseless violence impacted his life. After the attack his drinking increased. He drank more in order to blot out the horror that tormented him. His abuse of alcohol was affecting both his future with a security firm and his home life. As his wife was threatening to leave him, he was sinking deeper into quiet despair.

Two years after the bombing William was ordered by his firm into an inpatient program for alcohol addiction. In that program he was taught the disease model of alcoholism. He was also diagnosed as suffering from a delayed onset of post-traumatic stress disorder (PTSD) through which he was re-experiencing the trauma he encountered in Israel. The counselor advised him that his alcoholism was intensifying the PTSD episodes.

For five years William remained sober after leaving the program. During that time his work performance recovered. His marriage improved, though he still had occasional altercations with his wife. It was during an argument with her that William stormed out of his home in anger. In his confusion he chose not to return home but instead checked into a motel for the evening. That night he made two profound errors in judgment: he began to drink, and he missed his evening shift at work. Both of these errors came to the attention of his supervisor.

Although pleased with his recent performance, his company had a detailed record of William's alcoholism and PTSD diagnosis. Perhaps he was a *walking time-bomb*, or so they implied at his preliminary hearing. He was confused and discouraged, fearing the loss of both his job and his family. He had been a faithful member of the local church, and his pastor referred him to me. While actively listening to him, I had been waiting for an invitation to intervene with some suggestive questions.

"If only I could get some help," William said quietly, almost to himself. "My boss insinuated that I may no longer be of value to the firm since I'm an alcoholic and could still be suffering from PTSD. I think I have a great deal to offer. I've been doing a good job. If I could just get some help. I need some treatment!"

"Are you an alcoholic?" I asked.

"I guess so," William replied. "You never stop being an alcoholic, you know."

"Why do you think you are an alcoholic?" I responded.

William just stared at me, somewhat surprised. It had never occurred to him to question whether or not he was an alcoholic. This was the first issue that arose with his employer. Indeed, it was William who reminded his supervisor about the doctor's diagnosis of PTSD.

"Until now you haven't had a drink for over five years?" I asked perplexed.

"No, I haven't," he replied.

"How were you able to do this if you're an alcoholic?" I asked. "I mean, it must have been incredibly difficult, considering you say you are an alcoholic as well as suffering from PTSD."

"Well," William responded, "I jogged a lot and kept my mind on my job and family. But I haven't been able to do this very much any more since all these problems began. I just don't know what I'm going to do. I feel like I'm at the end of my rope. I've worked so hard to make my life work. I don't know what to do next. It's all falling apart. If I could only get some help."

"So you think you need to be in treatment?" I asked.

"Yes, if they would only let me," was William's immediate reply.

William's security firm viewed his insistence on going into a treatment program again as a sign of his inherent instability. William knew this, and it added to his frustration. At this point I decided to read Romans 8:28 with him.

"William, I want you to consider these words written by the apostle Paul. 'And we know that all things work together for good to them that love God, to them who are the called according to his purpose'" (KJV).

"What if," I suggested, "tonight while you are sleeping, this passage of Scripture came true for you? During the night a miracle occurred and the problems that brought you here to speak with me are solved. But you were sleeping, so you are not aware that this miracle has occurred. Tomorrow morning when you wake up, what will you notice that will tell you that this miracle has happened?"

"That's quite a miracle," William replied jokingly. "I guess I will be communicating better with my wife. She's always said that would take a miracle."

"Okay, you'll be communicating better with your wife." I agreed, smiling. "Tell me more about that. What would be different in your communication?"

"Well," William responded while slowly leaning forward, "I'm sure we wouldn't be arguing as much."

"What will you be doing if you're not arguing?" I asked, also leaning forward and with obvious interest.

"I guess we would be enjoying our time with each other," William replied.

"If I had a video camera," I asked, "and could see the two of you the morning after the miracle, what would I see you doing differently?"

"You would see me treating my wife with respect and love," William replied with a far-away look in his eyes.

"What will Cindy notice about you when you are treating her with more respect and love?" I wondered.

As I quickly jotted down some of his key statements, William went on to describe in greater detail how Cindy would know he loves and respects her. As he did so, he became more animated and excited about this possibility. I decided at this point to move beyond the marital relationship.

"What else might you be doing differently that would show you that this miracle had occurred?" I asked.

"I think I'd be treating other people with more respect too, and I would be more at ease," William replied.

Again, we discussed more specifically what he would be doing when he is treating others with more respect. As I jotted down the details, I asked, "So, when you are doing these things you will feel more at ease. What will be different when you're more at ease?"

"I'd feel more of God's peace, I'm sure of that," William replied.

"Well now, how will you know God's peace when you receive it?"

"I think I'd be more relaxed and at peace with myself," he answered. "But you know, I've never really thought about it that way before."

"Well then, what would Cindy and your children notice about you when you're more relaxed and enjoying God's peace?" I asked.

William went on to describe in some detail what his family would notice about him when this is happening, as I again made some quick notes.

"Let me see if I understand this correctly," I summarized. "You would be treating Cindy with more love and respect, which would greatly enhance your success in communicating; you would be showing more respect toward your fellow workers; and you would enjoy more of God's peace, thereby feeling more comfortable with yourself."

Wanting to establish William's willingness to work toward this possible vision of the future, I asked, "Imagine a scale of 1 to 10, with 10 meaning you have confidence that all the things you have described can be accomplished, and 1 meaning you have no confidence at all, probably because of alcoholism, PTSD, and possible loss of job and family. On that scale, where would you put yourself today?"

Shaking his head slowly William answered, "When I came in here I think I was at a minus 1!"

"Has something changed since you came in here?" I wondered.

"I'm not really sure," William said, shaking his head. "I guess I'm just hopeful that it can be fixed."

"Well, this is good news then, isn't it?" I said with a slight grin. "A miracle has happened, and it's fixed. So what's different now?"

William looked up and said, "My marriage is healthier and I'm happier." Then saying with emphasis, "I think I could be a 5 if I just had to take care of myself!"

"Wow, a 5! That's a lot more confidence!" I exclaimed. "What would have to happen to move you to a 5?"

"Well, I can't," he quickly replied. "It's not just me I have to think about; there's my family too."

"Does being a minus 1 help your family?" I asked carefully.

"No," William replied with a smile.

"Would being a 5 or even a 2 help your family?" I wondered, also smiling.

William replied, "Yes, it would." He was smiling now as if thinking of something for the first time.

So I asked another question. "William, let's consider another 1 to 10 scale. On a scale of 1 to 10, with 10 meaning you are doing all of these things we've been talking about to solve your problem and 1 meaning you'll just sit and wait for something to happen, where would you say you were before coming to see me today?"

"I think I was about a zero, I guess," he answered.

"And how about when you leave here today?"

"Well," he said slowly, "I guess . . . about a 5."

"That's terrific," I replied encouragingly. "So you are willing to do whatever it takes. Well, let's pause for a moment. I'd like to take a short break now to collect my thoughts and return with some feedback. Why don't you take a moment too, and consider any feedback you may have for me." William agreed.

At this juncture, we took a short break. After returning, I began by saying, "I'm very impressed that you took the time to confer with your pastor and then to make the trip all the way over here to talk to me. You are obviously willing to move forward, both for yourself and for your family. I'm also impressed with your insights regarding what will be different when you are on track.

"During the break I recalled a children's story called *The Silver Chair*. It was written by a man named C. S. Lewis. I had a copy of this book on my shelf and thought you might find this short portion of the story interesting. In this book there is a land called Narnia that was created by Aslan. Aslan is a powerful Lion who, in this story, is a type of Jesus Christ. The part I'm going to read starts with a young girl named Jill. She is very thirsty and is looking for water. In the distance she hears a stream. . . ."

> The wood was so still that it was not difficult to decide where the sound was coming from. It grew clearer every moment and, sooner than she expected, she came to an open glade and saw the stream, bright as glass, running across the turf a stone's throw away from her. But although the sight of the water made her feel ten times thirstier than before, she didn't rush forward to drink. She stood as still as if she had been turned to stone, with her mouth wide open. And she had a very good reason: Just on this side of the stream lay the Lion. . . .
>
> "If you are thirsty, you may drink," a voice said. . . .
>
> For a second she stared here and there, wondering who had spoken. Then the voice said again,
>
> "If you are thirsty, come and drink.". . .
>
> It was deeper, wilder, and stronger; a sort of heavy, golden voice. . . .
>
> "Are you not thirsty?" said the Lion.
>
> "I'm dying of thirst," said Jill.
>
> "Then drink," said the Lion.
>
> "May I—could I—would you mind going away while I do?" said Jill.
>
> The Lion answered this only by a look and a very low growl. . . .
>
> "Do you eat girls?" she asked fearfully.
>
> "I have swallowed up girls and boys, women and men, kings and emperors, cities and realms," said the Lion. It didn't say this as if it were boasting, nor as if it were sorry, nor as if it were angry. It just said it.
>
> "I daren't come and drink," said Jill.
>
> "Then you will die of thirst," said the Lion.
>
> "Oh dear!" said Jill, coming another step nearer. "I suppose I must go and look for another stream then."
>
> "There is no other stream," said the Lion.
>
> *C. S. Lewis, 1953, p. 19*

Then I asked William, "I wonder, has viewing yourself as an alcoholic and still suffering from PTSD been helping you?"

"It isn't helping, not really," he thoughtfully replied.

"Well, if it's not working," I suggested, "then perhaps you should stop viewing yourself in this way and try something different. You see," I continued, "in a sense, the 10 is the only stream you have. There is no other. Now if being an alcoholic and suffering from PTSD has been working for you, then continue doing whatever it is you're doing."

"I can be a 5," William said with confidence and still smiling.

"Let me know if I understand you correctly," I said. "When you are near a 10 you will be communicating more with your wife, treating her with respect and love." I went on to review some of the things I had jotted down, things that he had mentioned he would be specifically doing. "You will also be treating others with more respect as well as being more at ease and at peace with yourself." Again, we reviewed how he would be doing this.

"Well," I continued, "a 5 would certainly be on the right track to accomplishing this. Even a 2 would be movement in the right direction. Why don't you try acting somewhere between a 2 and a 5 this week and observe your family's reaction. Also, look for the good things that happen when you are doing this. Make a mental note of the things you're doing that work, and do more of that on purpose. Then, observe what is happening within you and around you when you're on track in this way. Consider what you're doing specifically. How do you feel emotionally when you are doing it? What do your friends and family notice that is different? Those kinds of things. Next week, come back and tell me about it. . . . Now, when you're doing a little of this, do you think you'll be on track toward getting what you wanted from coming in to see me this afternoon?"

"I believe I will be," William replied, now grinning. "I'm really glad I came in to see you today!"

COUNSELING AND THE PASTOR

As we can see in the above case illustration, the solution is not always derived from the problem. Indeed, the answer to the problem may have little to do with the problem itself. Most ministers and other Christian leaders I have met over the years are upbeat and positive individuals. They have a message of grace and power as well as of God's forgiveness and love. They seek to communicate strength and encouragement from God and the local church.

They are fully committed to their calling and preach a message of faith and hope every week. Teaching this message in Sunday schools, Bible studies, and adult elective classes is what they look forward to each week. Their sermons are new and fresh because they come from the very heart of God. As such they have seen a message wrap itself around an individual spirit in such a distinctive way that it works in each person's life uniquely according to God's will.

Yet as counselors they often experience frustration. They are expected to diagnose the problem, assess their own expertise, and determine the amount of time they have to give to those who approach them for help. Many feel they are not qualified to counsel the hurting individuals or families who come for help. The problems seem too overwhelming and complex. They listen compassionately, share Scripture, and try to offer options that seem right.

But many who come for help are hurt too deeply, and church counselors do not believe they are experienced enough to go any deeper into the cause of the distress. Perhaps the couple or family is too enmeshed or dysfunctional. There is too much anger or depression. Or there are issues that the counselor feels are simply beyond his or her capabilities. So they lovingly pray for them and then refer them to a professional counselor.

The professional counselor will also listen carefully but then will set up treatment goals based on the nature of psychopathology. And here is the rub. The nature and purpose of psychopathology are quite different from anything preached from the pulpit or taught in the classroom.

THE NATURE OF PSYCHOPATHOLOGY

The word psychotherapy comes from two Greek words. The first is *therapeutikos*, which means taking care of or attending to another. The second comes from the Greek word *psychē*, meaning soul or being. Thus psychotherapy means ministering to the soul or being of another person. The treatment of *mental illness*, by contrast, came out of the world of psychiatry. It is based on the concept of psychopathology, pathology being concerned with the nature of disease and its causes and development. Thus psychopathology refers to the *diseases of the soul.*

Psychopathology has been referred to by some as being flawed by a *deficiency language*, quite unlike the empowering language of Scripture. This "deficiency language has created a world of description that understands only through what is wrong, broken, absent or insufficient" (Goolishian, 1991, pp. 1–2). As we witnessed in the above story, William had become dependent and disabled by such descriptions.

DSM–4

One of the most influential books that encourages deficiency language is the *Diagnostic and Statistical Manual of Mental Disorders—Fourth edition*, or the *DSM–4*. As I said in chapter 2, this manual *gives structure to an entire way of perceiving reality*. It catalogs mental disorders and is the primary guide of the mental health community. Every professional counselor entering into a therapeutic relationship with a client, especially if that client is utilizing a third-party insurance provider for payment purposes, is required to make his or her diagnosis from the DSM–4.

Categories such as post-traumatic stress disorder (PTSD) and psychoactive substance-abuse disorders, which were mentioned in William's case illustration, as well as anxiety and mood disorders, sexual disorders, adjustment disorders, impulse-control disorders, and personality disorders are just a few of the many descriptions of mental disorders listed in this volume, and the list continues to grow.

There is no empirical support for any of the category classifications used in the DSM–4, by which each person is viewed pathologically through labeling and isolating. These categories were not developed to empower the counselee but to offer criteria for *describing* deficiency. As we saw in William's case, he had come to view *himself* as the problem. He *is* an alcoholic and is afflicted with PTSD. Once categorized in this fashion, the solution, finding and receiving the desired treatment, was no longer within William, but was now outside of his control. William's expertise and competency were never seriously explored, and he viewed himself as powerless to change. These are often the unintended results when a counselor uses deficiency language. One counselor spoke of a hypothetical day in the future when DSM–20 will come on the market with only one category: *STUCK*! At that time the goal of the counselor will be to simply help individuals get "unstuck"—a much more empowering approach, by the way.

Twelve Steps

Even the popular *Recovery Movement* is prone to this deficiency language. It is built on the philosophy of *Alcoholics Anonymous*, which holds to the disease model of addiction. It has now been extended to various other aspects of human functioning, such as overeating, gambling, and emotional or sexual behavior. This approach is very helpful in identifying outside support and in developing personal structure. It also *externalizes* the problem, calling it *alcoholism.* I will address the use and purposes of externalizing in a later chapter.

This approach is initially helpful but may later trap the individual into an unhelpful perception of himself. It often fails to identify the strengths, abilities, and goals of the counselee. Rather, his negative traits and problems become the primary focus. If the individual refuses to admit he is an alcoholic, this approach to therapy confronts him with being in denial and resistant to treatment. He may have little to say about his counseling experience, not even knowing specifically what the goal is.

In this case the counselee may be relying on the expertise of the counselor to guide him into some new self-understanding or insight that he hopes will reveal the reason for all his problems. Or he may be hoping to enter a program that will give him the strength he needs to master a certain inborn addiction. It is not my intention to speak disparagingly about anyone who is trying to help people, but I think there must be some room for healthy disagreement. In my opinion there is a rather captivating quality to all deficiency classifications and language: it makes room for the role of the expert.

The Expert

A common element within all psychopathological approaches is the utilization of an expert. An example of this approach can be found in a recent advertisement I received to subscribe to a mental health magazine. The letter is emblazoned with the words "Isn't your happiness worth just $1 a month?" Then when one opens the letter, he finds the answer to the first statement written in bold script across the top of the first page: "It's worth the small cost just to know you're really okay." In other words, let the experts tell you what is normal and what is not! It is assumed that what informs their decisions in this regard is established fact and therefore totally reliable.

A counselee may enter an initial interview with a reasonably clear view of his problem. Yet when encountering this expert approach, he is encouraged to believe in an underlying cause of which the supposed problem or problems are only symptoms. The expert is now in charge. He makes the evaluation and diagnosis. He sets the pace and clarifies the goals. Resistance to working toward these goals represents denial and self-sabotage.

In one sense it seems quite professional in scope. Treatment plans usually will include an initial diagnosis with objectives, proposed interventions, methods, possible need for medications, and prognosis. Directive or exploratory therapy will be considered, and the previous and present level of functioning of the counselee will be appraised. Yet *the strengths of the counselee are barely investigated, much less utilized.* Is not the counselee the expert on his own life?

It is not the competency of the therapist or support group that is at issue, rather it is the competency of the counselee. How has God already been at work in his life? What evidence is available to the counselor that can uncover this work of the Spirit? The professional therapist you may have sent your parishioner to with the best of intentions may actually focus on all the wrong issues. Thus problems are explored rather than solutions created. This form of deficiency language often leads to the certainty of *victimization*.

This is not to suggest that the church counselor need not be proficient. Anyone who wishes to counsel should receive training with qualified supervision. What is needed is skill regarding the *process of creating solutions* rather then relying on psychological knowledge regarding individual disorders, enmeshed relationships, or family systems. The solution-focused church counselor is skillful, *but his expertise is in the process of counseling, not in the "mental illnesses" of the counselee*. Toward the counselee we extend an abiding trust in God's sovereign intention.

God has left his imprint on every human life. We must find this evidence and use it in assisting the counselee toward God's intention. There may be reasons for ministers and other church counselors to refer to Christian psychiatrists and professional Christian counselors, yet making a referral too quickly signals to the parishioner that his problem is so bad that it is beyond the work of the Spirit and the fellowship of the church. This is sad indeed, for God intends to bring about lasting change and cognitive transformation.

Labeling

I have great respect for my colleagues in the psychotherapeutic profession. Their training is rigorous and their qualifications are difficult to attain. But training in deficiency conversation infiltrates much of their discussion regarding individuals who come to them for help. Although genuine illness is not a deficiency, some clients may be referred to *as* a mental disorder. "My borderline personality disorder is coming at 9:30," or, "I need some advice in working with my ADD." At issue is the intrinsic value of the client and the integrity of the therapeutic association with the therapist.

The DSM–4 is sometimes used to confirm a diagnosis with a counselee by reading the characteristics of a particular disorder. The purpose is to help the client identify what he is suffering from. Clients usually feel relieved, since they now know what they *have*. They can now get down to the hard task of working through their problem. One thing this approach assures is an unrestricted focus on the problem. The small percent of the client's life that represents the problem overshadows the larger percent of his life, which offers possible solutions. This approach also marks the counselee as personally deficient and therefore potentially reinforces the problem.

Along with labeling comes the danger of misdiagnosis, an unhealthy preoccupation with self, self-fulfilling prophecies, marketing abuses, and potential conflict of interest; e.g., the counselor gets paid more the longer the client stays in counseling. What is more, labeling can lead to the overuse of psychotropic mind-altering medications prescribed by psychiatrists or family doctors.

A COUNTERCULTURE

Christianity is in its truest sense a counterculture. That is, it is its own world—the entrance of the kingdom of God on earth, with all church leadership being in submission to Jesus Christ. It has its own mores and ethics, its own definition of value and success, its own community and support systems, even its own music and literature. Many within the church have become accustomed to going outside of this counterculture in order to obtain business opportunities, as well as education and medical care for their children. As the church becomes more acclimated to the present secular culture, some may also look within it for their entertainment and identity needs. The more Christians are at home in this present culture, the more they adopt its values and definitions of success.

The mental health community is right at home in the present culture. Indeed it is a fruit of it and defines all aspects of mental health from within its value system. As Christians become more comfortable with this current culture, it becomes easier for them to transfer their trust in the medical profession to trust in the mental health profession. They do not realize that the mental health community is still in a highly experimental stage. For example, it has been suggested that through its use of deficiency language it has constructed a world system of mental health—the world of mental health that I have referred to previously.

> This deficiency language has created a world of mental health that can be compared to a black hole out of which there is little hope of escape whether we are a clinician, theoretician, or researcher. In using the metaphor of the black hole, I am trying to capture the essence of a system of meaning whose forces are so strong that it is *impossible to escape out of the system and into other realities.*
>
> *Goolishian, 1991, pp. 1–2, italics mine*

This *world of mental health* is made up of characteristics that are often in conflict with Christian culture and values. Only with great care should a pastor or other Christian leader refer a parishioner into this "world." If referrals are being made, refer to Christian counselors and psychiatrists.

I find it intriguing that 95 percent of admissions to psychiatric centers and of personal psychotherapy sessions are for problems relating to depression and anxiety (Seligman, 1990). These are areas where pastoral competency is at its highest and where the Scripture is most outspoken. Even if the other 5 percent need to be referred to competent godly therapists and psychologists, it would still leave the vast majority in the care of the church.

Of course, this implies that the pastoral staff and elders will be doing the counseling. Where will these already overworked individuals find the hours to counsel effectively? Counseling is hard work. How are they going to handle the extra burden and stress of listening to the deepest problems of the congregation? And what if they make a mistake and hurt someone or make someone worse?

These fears are based on certain presuppositions that have been allowed to guide our thinking regarding counseling. Once these presuppositions are considered, new alternatives can be explored. The old ways of thinking regarding pastoral counseling just will not do. We have *new wine* in Christ, and this new wine should never be put into old wineskins. ■

CHAPTER FOUR

Hidden Presuppositions: Old Wineskins

"So tell me, what's the problem?"
"How long have you had this problem?"
"How do you feel about this problem?"
"Why do you think you have this problem?"
■ *Typical Counseling Questions*

"I've learned that if you stay focused on yourself, you are guaranteed to be miserable." ■ *H. Jackson Brown, Jr., 1991, p. 71*

Counseling has been categorized as being either directive or nondirective. This distinction has not proven useful. More likely counseling is always directive. For example, an approach once considered nondirective is *Client-Centered Therapy* by Carl Rogers (1951). Among other things, a client-centered counselor reflects back the words and ideas the counselee expresses. The counselor presupposes that this technique will help the counselee gain personal insights and increase his understanding of the problem. In so doing he leads the counselee back into his own thought processes. In this fashion he is *directing* the counselee. Another way counselors are directive is through the questions they ask.

Each of the questions at the beginning of this chapter directs the counselee's focus to a specific aspect of his problem and to the way the problem is affecting his life. But what presuppositions govern these questions? How do these presuppositions direct the counseling interview?

For example, the question "So tell me, what is the problem?" presupposes that there is a problem that must be understood. The question "How long have you had this problem?" presupposes that knowing the length of time the problem has been experienced will help lead to a solution. The question "How do you feel about this problem?" presupposes that problems cause feelings and that feelings need to be clarified in order to reach a solution. The question "Why do you think you have this problem?" presupposes that the problem has a cause and that finding it will help solve the problem. I believe these questions, although helpful for information gathering, carry with them the seed for deficiency conversation. These questions can be understood through two primary questions. The first asks why the problem exists.

WHAT IS THE ROOT CAUSE OF THE PROBLEM?

The question of the root cause of the problem proceeds from specific presuppositions. It presupposes that there is a specific problem, a precise cause to the problem, a relationship between the cause and solving the problem, and that when the cause is found and understood, the problem can be fixed. This is appealing. Most people like to get to the root of a problem; e.g., "Let's find out why the car is making that horrible noise and get it fixed!"

Unfortunately, in regard to counseling, the search for the root cause often intensifies and maintains the problem. The counselor's desire to ascertain the cause directs the interview into deficiency conversation. What if the counselee's problem is not a symptom of any deeper dysfunction? What if it is just a problem? Would it be acceptable to the counselee if his problem is resolved even though the "root cause" is never discovered?

> A common assumption of many traditional approaches to counseling is that there are deep, underlying causes not readily perceivable to the untrained eye that cause client complaints. Presenting complaints are seen as "symptoms"—only the tip of the iceberg. Indeed, the very word symptom implies that what clients complain of is not the "real issue" but only the outward manifestation of some underlying dysfunction. This iceberg theory comes from medicine, where treating symptoms can be inadequate or

> even dangerous. This, however, has been transferred to counseling based on tradition, not empirical evidence.
>
> *Huber & Backlund, 1993, p. 46*

In Christian theology the solution to personal sin is not found in understanding the root cause of sin, i.e., understanding the doctrine of original sin. Rather, it is through turning from sin to God's grace, being thankful for forgiveness, acting upon this forgiveness, and maturing within God's grace in a constructive and creative way.

Scriptural Admonition and the "Root Cause"

The church is the steward of biblical truth. Through preaching and teaching, church leaders want the local congregation to know this truth and apply it to their specific situations. Once the assembled believers are admonished regarding the scriptural teaching on a specific topic or problem and act on this truth, their problems are on the way to being solved. Scriptural admonition, or "nouthetic confrontation" (Adams, 1970), is an approach that uses a similar methodology. Its influence can be seen in many of the "biblical counseling" approaches available today.

However, what is good from the pulpit and within the classroom may not always be as effective in counseling. Often when individuals, couples, or families seek counseling, they are struggling emotionally and spiritually. They may not be willing or ready to hear this truth, especially when it forces them to confront possible sin. Although sin may be viewed as the root cause of many personal problems, discussion of the sin—that is, a focus on the problem—may not lead to a solution. Indeed, it may maintain the problem.

Also, truth must be applied in a context. In counseling, the context is often difficult to discern. To apply truth to an individual case accurately the counselor must be fully aware of all the details of the situation. He must also factor in his own assumptions and beliefs about the situation, or he may miss the mark. For example, consider Jay Adams's parable of the poor fellow sitting on a tack, with no one able to help him (1970, pp. 103–4): "Finally a nouthetic counselor comes upon the scene. He looks around and finds a tack under the client. He says, "'Get off that tack. Now that you're up, sit down on a chair over here and we'll talk about how you can avoid sitting on tacks in the future.'"

I enjoy this parable. It is a good story to tell from the pulpit in regard to taking specific actions. Yet in the counseling interview the "tack" may not be so easily identified. The counselor's perception of the tack may be different from the counselee's. The church counselor may determine that the problem is sin. Even if his judgment is correct, it leaves both counselor and counselee at an early impasse. A counseling session can become a battle of human wills. A stalemate may eventually come, no matter how skilled the counselor may be. It will come if the counselee continues in his sinful practices and is unwilling to change. But it need not be accelerated by the counselor.

One pastor told me how he had become frustrated with an older teenager who was sent to him by his parents. The young man was unresponsive and distracted during counseling sessions, seemingly uninterested in applying God's Word to his life. He consistently failed to complete assigned homework exercises. The pastor viewed him as difficult and disobedient, finally telling him so. After the counselee stopped attending, the pastor admitted to feeling uneasy about how the counseling ended. He then referred this family to a local counselor.

It is easy to second-guess this pastor. His choice to refer was correct, but I think his *paradigm* regarding what counseling is contributed to this premature impasse. What was the paradigm? In his case it was that Christian counseling is admonition from the Bible. The question I would ask is, *Whose goals were being addressed*, the pastor's or the counselee's? The teen needed help, and obviously the assignments were not meeting his need. The counseling approach of the pastor was not helpful. When something does not work in counseling, stop doing it and try something different.

In this instance the pastor's need to find the sin and admonish against it led to a confrontation. Confrontation, no matter how lovingly offered, is still disturbing. Most people are uncomfortable with it, and to assume that this discomfort is due to sin places the counselee in a double bind. To the counselee the confrontation sounds like this: "I'm the pastor, and I say your problem is a result of sin. I've shown you chapter and verse of the Scripture, so if you don't receive it, or if you're uncomfortable with it, that proves I'm right." Although few pastoral counselors would put it in these words, it comes through loud and clear to the counselee. When ministers and Christian leaders fail to consider their presuppositions, they can find themselves in difficult and often disturbing counseling sessions.

Cognitive Counseling and the "Root Cause"

The church counselor may have enough psychological education to utilize basic therapeutic techniques, putting some biblical verses into the conversation where suitable. But he often has little training or supervision with these techniques. If these approaches are problem-focused, which most are, they may once again maintain the problem.

Various therapeutic theories have been tried by pastors and pastoral counselors. The approach often used today is based on some form of Albert Ellis's rational-emotive therapy (RET) or one of the other cognitive-behavioral approaches. Approaches based on these theories are at the heart of most Christian counseling literature now available.

When the pastor asks, "So tell me, what is the problem you've come to talk about?" he is placing the focus squarely on the problem. When he asks, "Why do you think you have this problem?" he is putting the focus on how the counselee is thinking about his problem or problems. What is the root of the problem according to this approach? It is within the counselee's thinking. Yet, as anyone who uses this approach knows, when you seek to dispute the irrational beliefs of the counselee, you can get entangled into a morass of problems and misunderstood thoughts.

Such a pastor may need to confront the counselee during the interview, thereby showing more abrasiveness than many ministers are comfortable with. I believe one of the reasons pastors stop or limit their counseling is that it is too stressful. All they hear are problems, problems, and more problems. But if the pastor's goal is to change the counselee's thinking about the problem, he will need to know everything about it. I believe teaching and preaching are the most effective vehicles for the pastor to confront his congregation's sins and "irrational beliefs." Then this confrontation can take place within a loving body of believers where there is accountability, along with prayer and fellowship.

The second primary question refers to problem maintenance.

WHAT IS MAINTAINING THE PROBLEM?

The question of what is maintaining the problem also has its presuppositions. Instead of presupposing a root cause, this question presupposes that there is a problem that is being maintained. Problems are maintained by family structures, dysfunctional family systems, unwritten rules, styles of communicating, or even by that which the individual or family has been doing in an attempt to solve the problem. Yet the focus is still on the problem. The conversation within the counseling interview now focuses on what is maintaining the problem. The focus is on weaknesses within the system. Although there may be an actual "root cause" to a problem, we can see that awareness of it may not result in a counseling solution. In this way also, problems are often maintained. This approach has become quite popular; consider John

Bradshaw's PBS series on the family. But awareness in and of itself rarely produces a desired change. The counselee typically experiences months of therapy in learning about the dysfunctional structures, systems, rules, and styles. He may become expert on these concepts without drawing any closer to a solution.

Becoming Solution-Focused

Solution-focused pastoral counseling (SFPC) teaches that the counselee has all the resources he needs in God. The priority is to help the counselee get unstuck, not to generate personality change. True change occurs as a natural process of the sanctifying work of the Spirit. As we have seen, a question such as, "What is the root of the problem?" assumes that the solution is to be found somewhere deep within the problem. A question such as, "What maintains the problem?" assumes that the answer lies in present patterns that need to be analyzed, understood, and departed from. The question that underlies a solution-focused approach is, *"How do we create solutions with the counselee?"*

HOW DO WE CREATE SOLUTIONS?

The question of creating solutions also reveals presuppositions, but these presuppositions do not lead to deficiency conversation. They are: (1) God has given us the ability to create solutions, (2) the solutions can be described and clarified, (3) more than one outcome to counseling can be created, (4) the counselor and the counselee can do the creating and clarifying together, (5) we create solutions as a joint effort with God's preparation, and (6) this process can be taught.

Each of these presuppositions reflects a focus on solutions rather than on problems. The following story from Walter and Peller illustrate this approach.

> A few years back, during that rare year when the Chicago Cubs succeeded in winning their division championship, there was a time when one of the leading hitters was in a slump. Jim Frey, the manager of the team, spotted this hitter in the clubhouse one day. The hitter, with hopes of improving his performance, was watching films of himself up at bat. Now, you can probably guess what films he chose to watch. Right! He chose films of the times when he was in a slump, when he was striking out and generally doing everything but what he wanted. He, of course, was trying to find out what he was doing wrong so he could correct his mistake ... he was learning in greater and greater detail how to be a slump hitter ... (his manager complimented him on his commitment to the game and on his desire to improve himself) ... Jim then made one sug-

> gestion to the hitter—that he go back to the film room, find films from when he was really hitting the ball, and watch those films instead (1992, p. 5).

Jim Frey came upon this solution-focused approach quite naturally through his own experiences. When a church counselor uses this method, he *deliberately* does three things:

1. *Find out what the counselee wants.* Most people who come for counseling enter the session explaining what they do not want; that is, they tell you what their problems are. You may focus on these problems, unwittingly reinforcing them as you do so.

2. *Look for what God has already placed into the counselee's life that is working and encourage him to do more of that.* The approach of psychopathology is to diagnosis what is wrong and what is not working. This is something that every individual will have a different opinion about. In a solution-focused approach the church counselor is looking for what is working and then presents this as meaningful. This approach presupposes that God is actively engaged in the individual's life.

3. *Do something different.* You cannot dig yourself out of a hole by continuing to dig deeper. When what the counselee is doing is not working, it's time to try something new. God is always doing a "new thing" in our lives.

Once we leave the old wineskin of problem-focused counseling, this approach of describing and clarifying solutions offers a wonderful freedom for both counselor and counselee. Jesus predicted that "no one after drinking old wine wants the new, for he says, 'The old is better'" (Luke 5:39). Of course it is difficult to do anything in a new way; paradigms are hard to shift. Nevertheless SFPC implies that we can build solutions with a counselee, as the Holy Spirit guides the conversation. Building solutions is based in part on a constructivist view of reality. ■

CHAPTER FIVE

Meaning Is Perception: The Constructs That Bind Us

> We were talking about cats and dogs the other day and decided that both have consciences but the dog, being an honest, humble person, always has a bad one, but the cat is a Pharisee and always has a good one. When he sits and stares at you out of countenance he is thanking God that he is not as these dogs, or these humans, or even as these other cats! ▪ *C. S. Lewis, 1967*

It seems that Lewis was not partial to cats. Whether you are a cat person or a dog person, this tongue-in-cheek comment reveals something that many pet owners do; that is, we read human characteristics, emotions, and feelings into our pets. As we project these characteristics and qualities, we are constructing a view of reality for ourselves. Our perception of our pet becomes what is true *for us. Meaning is perception.* By this I mean that what we perceive to be true becomes true for us. This continues until a new perception challenges the first.

For example, three people observe a middle-aged man standing next to a young boy. He is raising his hand into the air. The first person says with conviction that the man is about to strike the small boy. The second says that this is not so at all. He is simply waving to his friend.

The third says with a shrug of the shoulders that the man was just stretching. Which opinion was true? Perhaps none. But each perception constructed an understanding of reality for the individual doing the perceiving. Therefore, perceptions exert a *forming influence* on us all.

In a practical sense, all of us construct reality, or what we believe to be true, for ourselves every day. Of the billions of individuals on earth, none is exactly like another. We are all "fearfully and wonderfully made" (Ps. 139:14). Every person lives in a world of his own creation. It has been constructed through his thoroughly unique experiences, life situations, reactions, choices, and genetic blueprint. Each has been, and is being, distinctively formed. Through personal faith and new birth we trust that this forming process is being orchestrated by God's Spirit.

This is not to imply that there is no absolute truth—only that absolute truth resides in God. We must guard against subjective relativity in regard to God's revelation and moral values. Yet we are all subject to the limitations of our humanity. As such we are learning to make sense of our surroundings and experiences. How we do so is important to the task of living and therefore to the task of counseling.

CONSTRUCTIVISM AND LABELING

Construction of individual reality refers to the constant process all of us are engaged in as we seek to make sense of what we experience each day. This way of understanding has been referred to as "constructivism" because it alludes to this process of constructing personal meaning (George Kelly, 1955).

> A constructivist perspective rests on the notion that all we really know about the world is our experience of it and the way me make sense of it. We are all engaged in a constant process of making sense of what we experience. Different things mean different things to different people. Some people regard things as problems that others find normal and acceptable . . . Nothing makes sense outside of its context, since the same event may mean different things if made sense of differently. The constructivist position suggests that it is the way things are made sense of that is the important element for therapy.
>
> *Durrant, 1993, pp. 3–4*

In contrast to this view, psychopathologists seek to label what is not fully knowable. The limitation of psychopathology is directly related to the uniqueness of the person it attempts to describe. Each person is a separate universe of ideas, memories, and feelings. Labeling *places meaning upon the counselee that actually flows from the counselor's or psychiatrist's own personal construct.* This can be, and often is, quite damaging to the counselee.

Perhaps when Jesus instructed humanity not to judge (Matt. 7:1), He did so because we are incapable of judging accurately. We use words to label what cannot be fully known by the assigned label. Often we see in others primarily what we have projected onto them. Thus the human propensity to use labels in the first place.

Labels such as liberal, conservative, fundamentalist, evangelical, catholic, main-line, chauvinist, feminist, enmeshed, dysfunctional, mood disorder, anxiety disorder, mental illness, gifted, and learning disabled are all used differently by different people. On the one hand we use labels to aid understanding and to find a common language for discussion. On the other hand we may pigeonhole, control, depersonalize, and discount individuals and ideas. All labels are employed to help the user *construct* a personal understanding of other people. Yet all labels are grievously flawed because of the uniqueness of the person being labeled and because of the human incapacity to judge correctly or to see others through the lens of God's grace.

So also in counseling. The counselor is bound, and therefore limited, by his own constructs. We all interpret through the lens of our personal constructs. We may unwittingly direct a counselee into an understanding of his personal situation or problem that actually reflects our own perceptions. Individuals so treated feel frustrated and misunderstood. This frustration may be read as denial or resistance by the problem-focused counselor.

SFPC, on the contrary, *cocreates solutions along with the counselee.* This is in keeping with the creative influence of the Holy Spirit, who is always in the process of creating solutions, moving us forward in our faith.

SUGGESTING A CONTEXT FOR CHANGE

Pastors and other Christian leaders are proficient in the art of suggestion. We seek to persuade through our preaching and educate through our teaching—all for the purpose of change. We suggest a life of faith and victory through our messages and our conversation.

Biblical truth is the heart of all preaching, teaching, and missions. *Truth represents more than doctrine. Rather, it embodies an entire way of perceiving, and living, life. The more firmly we hold to a belief, the more we are formed by the belief we hold.* It is truth that makes us free (John 8:32). This message of truth and the way we suggest it as being efficacious informs all our work as ministers. Our ability to suggest a life of victory and faith to our congregation, friends, and family must also inform our work as counselors, as we give personal attention to individual needs.

The difference is one of *methodology*, not of *intention*. From the pulpit our "methodology" is preaching and teaching. The "intention" of preaching and teaching is to consistently suggest that our life in Christ is an adventure and can be lived with a high degree of success and joy. This suggestion helps us to focus on eternal issues. We begin to see ourselves as sojourners during our time on earth. This is essential because *it is what we believe about the world to come that shapes how we live in the world today*!

This type of suggestion should also be the intention of counseling in the local church. Unfortunately, in the counseling interview the minister often departs from this fruitful approach, which he is comfortable and skillful with, doing so in the mistaken notion that counseling must focus on problems. Not only is he then no longer operating out of his strength, but also both his methodology *and* intention have changed.

A solution-focused counselor, by contrast, will guide but not control the counseling interview by his skillful use of questions. These questions are supported by his presuppositions. Although this is a different methodology, the *intention* is the same as that which supports preaching and teaching.

I do not believe that a focus on problems is the design of Scripture, nor have I ever heard any successful preachers or teachers whose primary intent is to explore problems from the pulpit. We quite naturally, and rightly, explore solutions from the Word of God. Even the most problem-oriented preacher has difficulty staying problem-focused in his preaching. The Bible simply does not permit it. It constantly focuses on the future and on solutions. These solutions—e.g., faith, grace, and hope—are often unrelated to the immediate problem.

If the minister will stay true to the intention of his preaching and teaching, he will be more solution-focused in his counseling. What is needed is a methodology to implement this intention. Ministers are already adept in the use of suggestion. Thus *the goal of counseling is to gracefully suggest the possibility of life without the problem.* What would be different if the problem were not there? This shift in focus to a future without the problem opens numerous new possibilities. Not only is it what we believe about the world to come that shapes how we live in the world today but also what we believe about our immediate future.

LIFESTYLE IDOLATRY

It is the design of Scripture that God should be at the center of our thoughts and dreams. When something takes God's place, it is a form of idolatry (Ex. 20:4–5). Our daily worship reestablishes God in His rightful place and in so doing reestablishes for us the authority lost in the Garden. Because *we are always formed by what is at the center of our lives* this is an issue of utmost importance.

If problems fashion the center of our daily existence, we are being formed by these problems. *If problems also fashion the center of the counseling relationship, the counseling is being formed by the problems as well.* Keep in mind, the constructivist view suggests that it is the way things are made sense of that is the important element for counseling. It is the counselee's view of his situation that stands in the way of finding solutions. It is the counselor's task to suggest a new way of making sense of the counselee's experiences. This is also in keeping with the way God's Spirit constructs or forms our individual identity. ∎

CHAPTER SIX

Identity Formation: The Unfolding of God's Grace

One of the reasons why it needs no special education to be a Christian is that Christianity is an education itself. ■ *C. S. Lewis, 1952*

Spirituality is not a life of suppression. That is negative. Spirituality is positive; it is a new and extra life, not the old one striving to get the mastery of itself. ■ *T. A. Sparks*

Forget the former things; do not dwell on the past. See, I am doing a new thing! Now it springs up; do you not perceive it? I am making a way in the desert and streams in the wasteland. ■ *Isaiah 43:18–19*

Psychopathology underscores a method of counseling that seeks to bring about insight through classification. It focuses on imperfections, weaknesses, and deficiencies—suggesting the inadequacy of the counselee. A solution-focused approach encourages positive change through an emphasis on outcome and a carefully described vision of a track to this outcome. It focuses on qualities, strengths, and abilities—suggesting counselee competency. Both approaches proceed from theories of identity formation.

DEVELOPMENTAL PARADIGM

How is personality formed? There have been many debates and theories about this question. The ancient Greeks developed philosophies that informed the debate for centuries. Every world religion has a belief system that includes a view on human personality. Freud's psychological theory of psycho-sexual development held sway during the early part of the twentieth century. At the present time it is Eric Erickson's theories that primarily influence the practice of counseling. Although he enlarged Freud's theory, Erickson stressed a psycho-social developmental approach. His paradigm has governed much of the discussion regarding the development of personality up to the present day. Erickson envisioned eight developmental stages to give structure to the formation of human personality. They follow through the entire life progression. Trust/Mistrust (age 0–1), Autonomy/Doubt (age 1–3), Initiative/Guilt (age 3–5), Industry/Inferiority (age 6–11), Identity/Role Confusion (age 11–18), Intimacy/Isolation (young adult), Generativity/Stagnation (middle age), and Integrity/Despair (old age). Each stage has both a healthy outcome and an unhealthy outcome. Scores of books and articles have been written by those who viewed personal identity development through this paradigm or one similar to it.

Erickson's theory assumes a linear view of existence; that is, one stage leads to the next. These classifications are intended to be descriptive, but they do represent a rather fixed view of human nature. When understood as tasks, they describe stages that need to be successfully completed before the human personality can move forward in a healthy fashion; thus an individual must go from *a* to *b*, and from *b* to *c*, in order to get to *d*.

Yet when this paradigm informs the counseling interview, it may result in presuppositions that actually hinder or limit forward movement. Perhaps the counselee learned to doubt at age two. Now the die is cast and his future is determined by these early experiences. The result for counseling is obvious. The counselee must go back and work through that stage more successfully, thus his need for insight. The result is to focus on the problems that hinder progress to the next stage.

Is it possible that God is not interested in, or limited to, these categories? We know He is beyond our linear view of existence. Through our relationship with Him can we move from *a* to *d*, incorporating the lessons from *a* through *c* in the process?

INTENTIONALITY

Any biblical view of how personality develops must be founded upon sin, separation from God, redemption, and new life. That is, it must be *founded upon God's grace and sovereign plan* for each individual life.

All human personality development begins with *God's intention.* Psychology and anthropology must be informed by theology. Little can be clearly understood when we start with humanity and human observation. This approach is what severely limits all humanistic theories of personality development. It is obvious that humanistic theories fall short when the message of Christianity is recognized as true history. At best, they describe a picture of human life apart from God.

Yet even this picture is unfinished. God is at work in each life in one way or another. He has specific plans for us to grow and to prosper (Jer. 29:11). His deliberate *intention* is for difficulty and evil to accomplish good for those who live according to *His intended purpose* (Gen. 50:20; Rom. 8:28). Those who harden their hearts still live within God's intention. From the same clay the potter can form some vessels for noble purposes and some for common use (Rom. 9:21). If an individual returns to God, he will be an instrument for His noble intentions (2 Tim. 2:21). God's intention for us becomes the formative truth regarding personality development, not primarily our understanding and perception of ourselves.

SPONTANEITY PARADIGM

This foundation of God's intention allows for true spontaneity. From a Christian perspective, that which seems spontaneous in our lives is actually the direct intention of the Spirit, who fills it with meaning. God is the author of all true originality, breaking into humanity and thoroughly disrupting all our theories and convictions.

God is doing a *new thing* in our lives (Isa. 43:18–19). He gives us a *new song* (Ps. 40:3), a *new name* (Isa. 62:2), and He makes a *new covenant* with us (Jer. 31:31). He gives us a *new spirit* (Ezek. 11:19) and a *new heart* (36:26). In Christ we are a *new creation* (2 Cor. 5:17) through a *new birth* (1 Peter 1:3) in which we put on a *new self* (Eph. 4:23–24). He will create *new heavens and a new earth* (Isa. 65:17). Indeed, He will ultimately make *all things new* (Rev. 21:5).

We are not to live in the past. Rather, we are to see ourselves as a new creation, created by God with a new heart and a new spirit, so that we may have the liberty to live in the new way of the Spirit. We are to continually put on our new self and to keep our eyes focused forward to a new heaven and a new earth. All of this reveals a spontaneous lifestyle, a walking in the Spirit (Gal 5:25). Although there is order in God's sovereign intention, it is concealed beneath the everyday life experience that we as Christians encounter in the freedom and spontaneity of faith. Regarding life experience C. S. Lewis wrote:

> What I like about experience is that it is such an honest thing. You may take any number of wrong turnings; but keep your eyes open and you will not be allowed to go very far before the warning signs appear. You may have deceived yourself, but experience is not trying to deceive you. The universe rings true wherever you fairly test it (Lewis, 1966).

The problem with secular theories of personality development is that they do not, and cannot, account for the intention of God for an individual's life. Nor can they account for the uniqueness of each individual. It is reported that Milton Erickson, a pioneer in the solution-focused therapeutic approach, once wisely said, "I do not have a general theory of personality development because I have never met a general person."

I am continually amazed at the diversity and uniqueness of those who come to me for counseling. To place a counselee into the black hole of labels, criteria, and classifications such as the DSM–4 is quite in opposition to this uniqueness. So also is allowing problem-focused presuppositions to limit the work of God's grace in the counselee's life.

IDENTITY-FORMATION PARADIGM

God's intention, which we view as it spontaneously unfolds in a life of faith, is the key factor regarding personality development. The choices we make, make us. We are constantly, and consistently, being formed by our choices.

> Most, I fancy, have discovered that to be born is to be exposed to delights and miseries greater than imagination could have anticipated; that the choice of ways at any cross-road may be more important than we think; and that short cuts may lead to very nasty places.
>
> *C. S. Lewis, 1969*

The story of David and Goliath is a biblical epic enjoyed by believer and nonbeliever alike. To some it represents courage and determination over brute force. To others it represents the victory of faith over seemingly insurmountable obstacles. Yet within this story we may overlook what *formed* David. What prepared David, as a teenager, to take on this challenge. Let's review the Scripture narrative. We enter the story with David speaking to King Saul:

> "Let no one lose heart on account of this Philistine; your servant will go and fight him." Saul replied, "You are not able to go out against this Philistine and fight him; you are only a boy, and he has been a fighting man from his youth." But David said to Saul, "Your servant has been keeping his father's sheep. When a lion or a bear came and carried off a sheep from the flock, I went after it, struck it and rescued the sheep from its mouth. When it turned on me, I seized it by its hair, struck it and killed it. Your servant has killed both the lion and the bear; this uncircumcised Philistine will be like one of them, because he has defied the armies of the living God. The LORD who delivered me from the paw of the lion and the paw of the bear will deliver me from the hand of this Philistine." Saul said to David, "Go, and the LORD be with you"" (1 Sam. 17:32–37).

It is at verse 38 that many preachers begin their sermons on David and Goliath, but for our purposes the most interesting information is given earlier. When David encountered the lion, he had a number of options, but let us narrow them down to two. He could hide or he could fight. The lion represents what I call a *grace event*. Grace events are the difficult battles—i.e., life situations—we encounter that help form our personality, usually without our knowing it. Afterward, we realize they were turning points. I refer to them as events of grace because *they represent the primary intention of the Holy Spirit for the Christian—to work upon our lives until "Christ is formed" in us* (Gal. 4:19).

Viewed from this side of eternity these grace events look a lot like problems and tragedies. So David, when he faced the lion, was facing, for the sake of illustration, a lion-sized problem. Yet from heaven's perspective, it was a grace event. If we could replay this encounter, allowing David two choices for each event, how would the outcome be affected? What we discover is the birth of a second David, with the grace event being the defining point, splitting the two.

Now if David had been my son, he would have heard my voice whispering in his ear, "You are more important to me than some sheep. Take care of yourself!" Indeed, it would have been common sense, from my way of looking at it, to do so. So let us say David hides from the lion, protecting his own life. Here is where the split takes place. We now have two Davids, the one who defeated the lion and the one who protected his own life. They have split at the grace event, i.e., the lion.

Let us assume that both Davids encounter a bear along their separate time lines. We know the first David defeats the bear. By contrast, there is good reason to believe the second David is going to protect his own life once again. He has been formed by his choice at the previous grace event. He must now act *without* this alternate experience. There has never been a reckless but courageous victory over the lion.

Now each David, in his separate time line, meets Goliath. In each case the problems have grown more threatening, but God's grace has also increased (Rom. 5:20). Both Davids hear the taunts and curses of Goliath. Both are outraged, but, as history records, the first accepts the challenge. The second stares, is angry, knows "someone" should do something, but stays behind the Israelite line where he is safe. He goes on to live a long, full life, eventually inheriting his father's flock, marrying, and living to a ripe old age. Then he dies and is remembered by his family for a few generations.

The David who accepted the challenge defeated Goliath, thus experiencing another encounter and a decisive victory through God's grace. This turning point is the third defining moment in his life. He goes on to become the most revered king Israel ever had, is loved and remembered by millions, and through his seed the *Son of David*, the true King and Savior of the world, is born.

So how does the human identity develop? From the light of the temporal mind there are stages to be worked through, problems to be analyzed, and emotional insights to gain. Much may be projected by the theorist onto the human race, and some of it does "seem" to be self-evident. But we have the mind of Christ (1 Cor. 2:16). From the view of God's intention we see *one consistent path, from birth through to eternity.*

Along that path God is working *all* things for good for those who are his and who walk in agreement with his purpose (Amos 3:3; Rom. 8:28). He is *forming* us according to His intention and plan. We are being transformed into his likeness (2 Cor. 3:18). Therefore, the formation of Christian identity is truly a study of God's grace. It is the Spirit who clarifies a person's identity, with the intention that that person become a son or daughter of God.

AGREEMENT WITH THE SPIRIT'S INTENTION

What is the implication for counseling? We know that we must be in agreement with God's intention for our lives if we wish to walk with Him (Amos 3:3). It seems simple enough, yet I believe it is the *key* to all identity development. Inasmuch as counseling is in agreement with God's intention for the counselee, it will be effective. Each person has his own path, or track, by which the Spirit is leading him. More often than not the counselee is not specifically aware of this guidance, much less is the church counselor. Yet a continuous flow of God's grace is forming each believer.

But we are assured that the Spirit has begun this forming work within the counselee and intends to complete it (Phil. 1:6). God's love, God Himself as He truly is, is being formed in us and is forming us. And He has pledged to carry His goal of formation through to its completion. His love is made complete in us (1 John 4:12).

> What, then, is the difference which He [Jesus] has made to the whole human mass? It is just this; that *the business of becoming a son of God, of being turned from a created thing into a begotten thing, of passing over from the temporal biological life into timeless 'spiritual' life, has been done for us* . . . If we will lay ourselves open to the one Man in whom it was fully present, and who, in spite of being God, is also a real man, He will do it in us and for us.
>
> *C. S. Lewis, 1952*

Do we as counselors really believe this? Or do we believe that the counseling interview is solely dependent upon our own wisdom and ability? This trust in our own understanding is what I believe results in most counselor burnout. So what is the relevance of all this for counseling? It is exactly this—*to help the counselee get on track in regard to the formation process that is* already *in place.* It is to have faith in the Spirit's intention and to be in agreement with His spontaneous manifestation.

If we keep in mind the constructs that bind us and often blind us as counselors, we will be more aware of what a difficult task this can be. If all counseling is directive, how can anyone trust himself or herself to counsel? If the counselor is influenced by his own constructs, as all counselors are, how can he ever find agreement with God's single "consistent path from birth through eternity" for the counselee? It seems that the counselor would need to be all-knowing.

It has been said that life is what happens when you are busy doing other things. This is meant to be humorous, but it contains a subtle truth with implications for counseling. In problem-focused counseling the emphasis is on the "other things"—that is, the problems that so occupy our attention and use up our time. In SFPC the emphasis is on the "life" that seems to be slipping by unnoticed and, more important, unappreciated.

If you could see the counselee's life from God's perspective, you would see evidence of His presence clearly upon it. Grace-events, strengths, *all point to possible exceptions to the present problem.*

Thus David's grace-event encounters with the lion and the bear helped form him. This formation prepared him to face Goliath and other challenges beyond. Yet if he had focused on the size of this problem, he might still have forgotten his strengths. He might still have been overwhelmed by his *fear* of Goliath. His counselor could have focused on David's fear of Goliath, thinking that if David could learn more about his fear he would be able to defeat the giant. Yet the more time he would have spent exploring his fear, the greater his fear would have become.

Instead, the counselor could have *suggested* strength by asking *when* David, either in his past or in recent weeks, had *not* had this fear. This question assumes that there are times when fear is not in control. David would then have recalled the events of God's grace *that were already in place in his life.* The counselor would not have known about these exceptions to the problem, only David and the Lord were experts on David's life. The Spirit had already put the evidence of His presence in place, just waiting to be discovered and expanded upon.

"So, what was different about those times, David?" the counselor might have asked.

"Well, I went after the wild beasts, struck them, and rescued the sheep from their mouths. When they turned on me, I seized them by their hair and struck them down." Now David would be getting back on track with God's intention.

"How is that different from the way you are facing Goliath?" The focus is not on the fear but on the solution to that fear.

The solution-focused counselor is in agreement with the Spirit's intention when he focuses on strengths or exceptions to the problem and when he is cocreating with the counselee a vision of life without the problem. The counselor's purpose is to help the counselee *get unstuck and back on track with the Lord.* All the problems are viewed from within the context of the ongoing work of the Spirit.

Counseling in this fashion is both fun and serious at the same time. It is fun because the focus is on the work of the Spirit in the counselee rather than on the potentially consuming problems. It is serious because it *is* possible to miss the grace of God (Heb. 12:15). It must be deliberately looked for. Once it is discovered, the counselee can declare along with Lewis, "I believe in Christianity as I believe that the sun has risen: not only because I see it but because by it I see everything else" (1952).

THE ISSUES OF LIFE

Being in agreement with how our identity is actually formed is crucial, for from this flow the issues of life (Prov. 4:23). We *are* being formed. We can choose Baal and become like Baal, or we can choose God and become like God. As the prophet Hosea wrote of Israel, "When they came to Baal Peor, they consecrated themselves to that shameful idol and became as vile as the thing they loved" (Hos. 9:10).

But we must deliberately be aware of our choices. All issues of justice and social responsibilities flow from who we are. We are being formed even *as* we form; there is a constant interaction. We are taken by what we take. What we believe in we become.

The Bible is a record of humanity's encounters with God. It describes His entrance into human history. It records *grace events* and the *writing of the Spirit* in numerous lives. It is given to teach us to be tenacious about the things of God and to develop a mature hope in His intention (Rom. 15:4). This is true as well of our own lives. Everything that was written in our past by the Spirit was written to teach us. Thus, in his book *The Great Divorce* C. S. Lewis speculates that heaven works backwards. That is, as we draw closer to the Spirit's intention for our lives we begin to see that His handwriting can be discovered upon our lives from birth (1946).

Theological grace can be easily received—and abused. Much of Christian religion is built around this sad fact. *Forming grace*, by contrast, is consistently life-challenging and transforming, abused only at the greatest personal risk. Grace reveals God's power (2 Cor. 12:9), and it is the very environment in which we are to grow (2 Peter 3:18). As Aslan said to Jill, "There is no other stream."

THE GOAL OF SOLUTION-FOCUSED PASTORAL COUNSELING

In its broadest sense the goal of all mental-health professionals is to help people feel better about themselves and their lives (Seligman, 1991), but this is not God's primary goal for His children. The goal of God's grace is to produce spiritual fruit, resulting in righteousness toward God and man (Matt. 22:36–39; John 15:5–8; Gal. 5:22–23). Feeling better about ourselves and our lives is a by-product of fruitfulness, just as happiness is a by-product of joy.

The apostle James, the son of Zebedee, laid aside economic power; Paul laid aside religious and political power; Matthew Levi laid aside wealth and personal pleasure. All gave their lives for the gospel. I doubt that their goal was to feel better about themselves—even though the fruit of their obedience was peace from God, which exceeds all attempts to understand it (Phil. 4:7).

When it comes right down to it, this fallen world is simply not conducive to mental health. Although Christians certainly want to feel better about themselves and their lives, feeling better is not our primary goal. Indeed, this desire of the mental-health community may be unattainable for Christians, who should always feel some unease because they are living in this present fallen world (James 4:4).

Our minds are on the eternal realities. Our peace is a result of abiding in Christ—not simply thinking good thoughts. Psychology states that spirituality "may" be a component of good mental health. Christianity teaches that mental health is just one component of spirituality, i.e., life led by the Spirit (Gal. 5:16, 25; 1 John 2:6).

Therefore, Christian counseling enters into this work of the Spirit as *He* is forming the unique identity of the counselee. Preaching, Christian education, and supportive fellowship all contribute to this same intention. Counseling has no unique agenda. It is simply a continuation of the work of the Spirit. The only difference is one of methods; the intention is the same.

Yet it is also important to understand some contrasts between counseling, preaching, education, and support. Although God's intention remains constant, the methods that support His intention *are* different. For example, the method of preaching is to persuade the listener to receive the purpose and plan of God. The method of Christian education is to teach the student to apply spiritual knowledge. The method of supportive fellowship is to develop relationships that offer encouragement, mutual sharing, and strengthening. And the method of counseling is to cocreate between the Spirit, counselor, and counselee a solution-oriented focus, to clarify that vision, and to facilitate that process. Each method promotes God's intention.

SFPC is educational in that it draws out of the counselee's own life experiences new ways of viewing the work of the Spirit—e.g., the past grace events, strengths, and exceptions. It is not educational in the sense of being primarily instructional or offering explanations and advice. If a counselee is seeking marital enrichment, he should be directed to a workshop, seminar, or marriage retreat. If he wishes to strengthen parenting skills, a parenting class should be offered. But going to a workshop or class is different from counseling.

Support is also distinct from counseling. As we will see later, the church counselor must be an attentive listener, but this is listening with a specific purpose. Support and encouragement are a part of counseling but are not the goal of counseling. Indeed, *mere support may encourage an unhealthy dependence* on the counselor. In the counseling interview ways may be considered by which the counselee could develop a healthy support system of friends, family, and church fellowship, but counseling should not be primarily supportive.

If the individual, family, or marriage is in a perceived crisis or presents a gradually escalating problem, then counseling is in order, with education and support strengthening the gains made in counseling. When support or education become the focus of the counseling session, the counselor is working too hard to sustain the counselee. He is actually doing the counselee's work, trying to emotionally uphold him.* As many ministers have discovered, this approach can become a full-time responsibility. Perhaps this is one reason why pastors tire of counseling and refer counselees to professionals outside of the local church.

THE CHURCH

Earlier I mentioned the "black hole" of deficiency language that reflects the world of mental health at the present time. In astronomy a black hole is speculated to be a collapsed star with an intense gravitational field. Even light cannot escape, thus its name. Likewise, once a counselee enters the mental-health world that focuses on deficiencies it is difficult to escape from it. It is populated by well-intentioned experts who often claim to know more about you than you know about yourself. Legal courts will place more credence on expert opinion than on an person's own personal beliefs.

But what is really needed to help a person in distress? Miller (1995) reports that all effective counseling approaches share four common factors. His research reveals that the first and most critical is extra-therapeutic—that is, *what the counselee brings to counseling.* This includes his preexisting strengths and abilities as well as chance events that may have an impact on him. The second factor is the quality of the *counselee's participation in counseling*. Empathy, respect, genuineness, and a thoughtful appreciation of the counselee's situation were vital contributions from the counselor's part of the process.

The third factor is the counselee's sense of *hope and expectation for success*. This happens when the counselor "speaks" the counselee's language and can adopt his frame of reference. Fourth

---

*An exception to the rule is an initial pastoral visit to someone who is grieving. This visit should be more supportive than directive or educational. If a reasonable time has elapsed and grieving has become unhealthy (1 Thess. 4:13), the individual may have become stuck in his or her grief. In such a case, counseling is once again appropriate.

and, interestingly, least important, is the counseling model and theory. Of these, Miller found that the most effective were those that *focused on what was happening outside of counseling and on encouraging responsibility.* All of the above are contrary to long-term problem-focused therapy.

These factors are clearly represented in pastoral counseling, specifically that offered from within the reassuring environment of the local church. Here is where I believe the church truly shines. Many have felt impoverished through their dependence on the secular mental-health system. They have experienced the tugging of the black hole. It is refreshing to discover that personal faith in Christ and lively association in a healthy local church really offer a way out.

A genuinely caring church counselor can learn to utilize the counselee's preexisting strengths and "chance" events. He can encourage rather than hinder the change that the Spirit is planning. The church counselor has God's Spirit to assist in regard to empathy, genuineness, and *hearing* the counselee's concerns. Hope is the heart of God's revelation that the church counselor brings to a counselee. Indeed, counseling is a sacred moment when one spirit touches another, supporting faith and emotional growth.

Supporting the counseling process is the loving and encouraging fellowship of the local church. This fellowship is the antithesis of deficiency language and the world of psychopathology and mental health. *Within the doors of a committed and healthy church are caring discipleship classes; men's and women's groups in which accountability to and for one another is fostered; classes for biblical studies; sermons that motivate, persuade, and convict; social involvement; mentors; and two or three vital, close relationships.*

I am reminded of the story of the pastor who was ill in bed one cold Christmas day and had to miss the Christmas Eve service. He heard the singing from his parsonage and decided to bundle up against the cold and just peek in for a moment from outside the church window. It was dark and miserable outside. The wind was bitterly cold, and he felt so very alone. As he approached the window, he was deeply stirred by the contrast. It was dark and cold outside, but within, bathed in the glow of God's light, were Christian friends, their hearts lifted up in song. All of a sudden he was struck by the enormity of the plight of the lost. *This must be what it is like to feel empty and separated from God*, he thought—*to look into the heart of heaven without entering in.*

This story brought home for me the vast difference between the world of mental health and the life of the church. Of course it is dangerous to generalize. Few things are entirely black or white. On the one hand, there are churches devoid of the life of the Spirit and ministers who are uncaring and sometimes corrupt. On the other hand, there are deeply caring and loving professional therapists; indeed most of those I have met I would describe in this way. My point is that the church contains within it all that is necessary for emotional strength and hope for the future. Professional therapy, at its best, is a pale imitation of the Lord's church.

It is the intention of the Spirit to form the unique identity of the counselee while he is within the love and support of the local church:

> In fact God has arranged the parts in the body, every one of them, *just as he wanted them to be* . . . those parts of the body that seem to be weaker are indispensable, and the parts that we think are less honorable we treat with special honor. . . . But God has combined the members of the body and has given greater honor to the parts that lacked it, so that there should be no division in the body, but that its parts should have equal concern for each other. If one part suffers, every part suffers with it; if one part is honored, every part rejoices with it. Now you are the body of Christ, and each one of you is a part of it. . . . His *intent* [is] that now, through the church, the manifold wisdom of God should be made known to the rulers and authorities in the heavenly realms.
>
> *1 Cor. 12:18, 22–28; Eph. 3:10* italics mine

"It was [Christ] who gave some to be apostles, some to be prophets, some to be evangelists, and some to be pastors and teachers, to prepare God's people for works of service, so that the body of Christ may be built up until we all reach unity in the faith and in the knowledge of the Son of God and become mature, *attaining to the whole measure* of the fullness of Christ" (Eph. 4:11–13, italics mine). This is "God's household, which is the church of the living God, the pillar and foundation of the truth" (1 Tim. 3:15).

It is with great care and caution that any Christian leader should refer a counselee to someone outside of the local church to get professional counseling from a system that may lack the loving, forgiving, empowering, and supportive environment of the body of Christ. ■

CHAPTER SEVEN

Guiding Assumptions: A Way of Thinking

When the servant of the man of God got up and went out early the next morning, an army with horses and chariots had surrounded the city. "Oh, my lord, what shall we do?" the servant asked. "Don't be afraid," the prophet answered. "Those who are with us are more than those who are with them." And Elisha prayed, "O LORD, open his eyes so he may see." Then the LORD opened the servant's eyes, and he looked and saw the hills full of horses and chariots of fire all around Elisha. ■ *2 Kings 6:15–17*

Sometimes our way of thinking limits what we can see. We make assumptions that limit our capabilities—or the capabilities of others. ■ *Charles Allen Kollar*

I heard a story that went something like this: Once upon a time there was a motorist, driving on an unlit back road late at night. When the thought entered his mind that he would hate to break down in such a dark and lonely place, a tire went flat. As he pulled his car quickly to the side of the road, his headlights lit up a sign that read, "Glenville Mental Institution." The motorist got out of his car to check for damage, but he had an odd feeling that he was not alone. Someone was peering through the nearby fence of the institution, not saying anything, just watching.

After taking off the flat tire, the owner of the car put the five lug nuts in the hubcap so they would not get misplaced. The stranger was still watching, and the motorist was getting nervous, now convinced that someone was staring at him from behind the fence.

What's a maniac doing out so late at night? he thought. *And why is he gawking at me like that?*

While rolling the spare tire around from the trunk he stepped on the rim of the hubcap, flipping all the lug nuts into the tall weeds. He went after them but found only one.

Finally, the mental patient spoke: "Take one nut from each of the other wheels and put them on the fourth wheel. Then you'll have four nuts on each wheel and be able to get to a gas station."

The motorist replied, "That will work." Then, "Hey, that's brilliant! What in the world are you doing *here*?"

The patient said, "I'm here because they think I'm crazy, not stupid."

When it comes to counseling within the local church, it cannot be overemphasized that one's *beliefs* about counseling are as important as one's knowledge and skills. Learning the difference between a problem-focused approach and a solution-focused approach is a start. When this paradigm shift takes place, a new way of thinking about counseling begins.

We have considered presuppositions and how they can direct the counseling interview, often without the counselor's knowing it. As stated earlier, SFPC has its own presuppositions: (1) God has given us the ability to create solutions; (2) the solutions can be described and clarified; (3) more than one outcome to counseling can be created; (4) the counselor and the counselee can do the creating and clarifying together; (5) we create solutions as a joint effort with God's preparation; and (6) this process can be taught.

The following are guiding assumptions that proceed from these presuppositions. (Some of these assumptions are adapted from de Shazer, 1988; Walter & Peller, 1992; Selekman, 1993; Durrant, 1993.) Together, they offer the counselor a new paradigm for counseling. They are basic to the practice of solution-focused pastoral counseling and offer a practical and healthy approach to the problems brought to the church counselor.

GUIDING ASSUMPTIONS

1. God is already active in the counselee.
2. Complex problems do not demand complex solutions.
3. Finding exceptions helps create solutions.
4. The counselee is always changing.
5. The counselee is the expert and defines goals.
6. Solutions are cocreated.
7. The counselee is not the problem, the problem is.
8. The counseling relationship is positional.
9. The counselor's focus is on solutions.

1. GOD IS ALREADY ACTIVE IN THE COUNSELEE

It is essential to keep in mind that God has been, and continues to be, thoroughly involved in the counselee's life before we, as counselors, try to help. God is active in the heart, mind, and spirit of all who will ever come to know and love Him. At issue is whether we who are counselors within the local church are going to trust what God has already been doing in the counselee. SFPC assumes that the counselee is capable of knowing and doing what is necessary to move toward God's intended outcome for his problem and for his life. All of us can do whatever is necessary through the strength we receive in Christ (Phil. 4:13).

When we assume God's activity, we begin to look for clues of this activity. We presume they are there. Recent changes, the writing of the Spirit, grace events, strengths, exceptions to the problem—all help us uncover what the Spirit has prepared. There are capabilities within the counselee that can be unearthed to help him in creating a solution. Focusing on these capabilities and building on them is of greater assistance than focusing on problems.

Not long ago Joshua, a distressed father, came to see me regarding his son David. David was being released from a psychiatric center the next day, and his father needed help in dealing with this family crisis. I listened attentively as he told his story, interrupting only to note strengths and capabilities.

David was twelve years old and overweight. His parents had divorced last year, and three weeks ago David moved in with his dad. Shortly after his son moved in, Joshua found a kitchen knife under his son's pillow. He also discovered notes in his drawer that described acts of violence. Joshua was concerned about this as well as about the music David was listening to, as the lyrics encouraged violent acts.

After Joshua consulted with social services, David was taken to a local hospital and from there to the psychiatric center. The staff psychiatrist recommended inpatient treatment. David was diagnosed as having an attention deficit disorder (ADD) and being in the midst of a major depression. Both are legitimate diagnoses within the world of mental health, yet both also limit further search for strengths. The doctor prescribed the psychotropic drug Prozac for depression and Ritalin, a stimulant, for ADD. David remained as an inpatient for seventeen days. His father was informed that David was most likely genetically predisposed to depression. Throughout his stay David remained angry with his father and begged to be brought home. The experts advised against it.

As I listened to this story I had the sensation of a great black hole spinning in space. It was drawing this family into its vortex. With the best of intentions the mental health system, from the initial contact with the social worker to the ultimate hospitalization, led this trusting family into its whirlpool of mental diseases, victimization, and mind-altering medications.

There is no doubt that David's behavior had been deteriorating. He felt angry, powerless, and hopeless. His world, like Humpty Dumpty, had broken to pieces, and he did not know how to put it back together again. Nothing within the present approach to treatment was empowering him to do so. Indeed, the diagnosis and treatment made it clear that David was not responsible for his behavior. He had a disease. At no time did any professional within the mental health system focus on family capabilities. Their problem-focused paradigm kept them from looking for any.

Nevertheless, when I listened to his story I assumed God was already active in the life of this family. It was my responsibility to act on this belief, looking for clues of His activity and preparation. I did not need to look far. Joshua was eager to do anything that would help. Nothing like the incidents with the knife and the notes had occurred previously. In fact, there were numerous *exceptions* to this behavior.

Joshua described how he had recently sat with his son and, while hugging him, told him how much he loved him. I asked if this had helped his son, and he said it had. In fact, it was a wonderful memory for him. As the interview progressed, many strengths and capabilities were revealed in this concerned and loving father. I began to wonder what his son's strengths were. No one else had been interested in David's capabilities or in what *he* wanted.

In the supportive feedback portion of the interview I told him how impressed I was with his love and dedication to his son. I then explained to him how every child has an *emotional tank* (Campbell, 1993, p. 33). This tank is filled by loving and accepting eye contact, appropriate touching, and focused attention, and I complimented him on doing this with his son. I encouraged him to continue his physical expressions of love, since these were what had helped his son the most.

I explained that it is possible to love our children without their *feeling* loved. Our goal must be for our children to *feel* loved, especially when they are in the midst, as David was, of a distressingly confusing time in their lives. The emotional tank needs to be filled with good experiences. When this tank is not filled, or is in need of filling, various problems begin to be manifested. Focusing on correcting these problems is a fruitless enterprise if the tank remains unfilled.

To illustrate, I asked Joshua to consider his automobile. What if your car engine stalled, and you were stranded in traffic? After your car was towed to a garage, a mechanic examined it in order to discover the problem. He gave it a full tune-up, but still the engine would not start. The electrical system was checked, much of it being replaced, still without success. Finally, the mechanic replaced the engine. Even then the car would not start. Later another mechanic suggested checking to see if there was fuel in the tank. Of course, it was empty. Once the car's tank was filled, and the key was turned, the engine started right up.

We would all agree that the first mechanic had been absurdly negligent. All this time and money to fix a car, when it was simply out of gas. Yet we often look for reasons for the problems we have with our children, and our efforts demand a great deal of expense and time. Often the approach the experts recommend for fixing the problem becomes part of the problem. With children, a large portion of the solution is right before us—it is to fill the child's emotional tank.

Joshua said he would do more of this when his son came home. I encouraged him to do so and to make a mental note of what happened when he did. Eventually I saw Joshua, along with David, three more times. Without giving details of what happened during the sessions, I can say that the end result was a family back on track. I continued to encourage father and son to do more of the things they described to me as being helpful and, like detectives, to try to catch each other doing these things. I continued to compliment them on their successes and strengths, as well as helping them describe and stay on track toward their goals. Eventually, they became a team, the goal being to stay on track together.

At this time both father and son are active in a local church and growing in Christ. Joshua is spending as much of his time as possible cementing his relationship with his son.

We always find what we are looking for. If a counselor looks for signs of ADD, he will find it. When he looks for a dysfunctional family, he will find that as well. When a counselor looks for deficiencies, he will always find them—since we *all* have deficiencies to one degree or another. SFPC prefers not only to look for strengths but also to assume they will be there as part of the sovereign work of God.

This reminds me of an interesting experiment by D. L. Rosenhan, a professor of psychology and law at Stanford University. He had eight emotionally healthy people, himself included, admitted to twelve different psychiatric hospitals. The psychiatrists who were assigned to these "patients" were simply told that they were "*hearing voices.*" Each patient gave a thoroughly honest statement regarding his mental state. Even though each would have been considered normal by any standard of society, each was diagnosed as *schizophrenic.* One was also diagnosed as *bipolar (manic-depressive).*

Keep in mind that each "patient" acted normal. Yet, once they were viewed as mentally ill, their normal behavior was perceived as a pretense—masking abnormality. Each was held from between seven to fifty-two days. A total of over 2,100 pills were administered to this group of patients. Rosenhan eventually informed the hospitals of his actions. He also advised them that he would try to do the experiment again in the near future. What was the result? Of the next 193 admissions, the staff found 41 impostors. It is interesting that Rosenhan had not repeated the experiment (Striano, 1987, p. 79).

It is simply human nature to do what these psychiatrists did. Even the most objective and professional of us will usually see what we are looking for. That is why it is so essential to be looking for strengths and competency. Since we assume God's intention for the counselee is good, and that He has been preparing him for spiritual and emotional health, we should be looking for evidence of His activities.

In the prophecy of Jeremiah, we read, "This is what the LORD says: 'Stand at the crossroads and look; ask for the ancient paths, ask where the *good way* is, and walk in it, and you will find rest for your souls'" (Jer. 6:16, italics mine). We are to look for these ancient paths when we come to the crossroads in our lives. The ancient path is the *good* way. It is the way that is both healthy and helpful. In the midst of our options, the ancient and true choice will always be the one that leads us home to God.

When we assume God's activity, the only reason for looking into the counselee's past is to assist him in *getting back on this good way.* This is the path that reveals God's peace and blessing. As the counselee begins to reconstruct this path, he can return to it. The crossroad could represent the counselee's being emotionally or relationally stuck. Within his past experiences, strengths will be revealed that have been unintentionally discarded. Return to this good way where God has been active, and new possibilities for solutions will be made manifest.

2. COMPLEX PROBLEMS DO NOT DEMAND COMPLEX SOLUTIONS

I once received a phone call from a woman who was quite distressed about her marriage. Unable to see her that day, I asked her to think of all the things in her marriage that were working, that is, that she wanted to have continue. She was to develop a list, and we made an appointment for early the next week.

A few days later she called and canceled the appointment, saying that she had taken my suggestion to heart. To her surprise she had made a rather lengthy list of the things that were going well in her marriage and that she wanted to see continue. She concluded that she wanted to give her marriage another chance. She thanked me for "being so helpful," and I let her know that I was available if she needed any assistance in the future.

Not being able to see a person immediately sometimes presents a difficulty. I approach this difficulty in a way that is similar to what has come to be called the *Formula First Session Task*, or *FFST* (de Shazer & Molnar, 1984, p. 298). The *FFST* approaches the counselee in this way: "Between now and the next time we meet, I would like you to observe your family so that you can describe to us next time what happens in your family that you want to continue to have happen."

This is a task that has been used by de Shazer to prepare his clients for their first counseling session. It is based on the belief that *no matter what the problem that is bringing individuals into counseling may be, that problem does not happen all the time.* There are other times that are good. There are aspects of their lives that they are happy with. The wife who canceled her appointment with me said that she suddenly realized things were not that bad. She was going to wait awhile and see what happens next. She also decided, on her own, to show her list to her husband and to encourage him to make his own list. I thought that this was a wonderful idea and encouraged her to stay on track with this more positive approach to her marriage, i.e., to find out what is working and do more of it.

A church counselor may say that this is just the old approach of telling someone, "Count your blessings." But there is a key difference. The SFPC approach *assumes* that there are things that the counselee would like to have continue. This is a subtle but powerful *suggestion* that compels the counselee to shift paradigms and look at the situation from a totally new perspective. If we state the obvious, e.g., "count your blessings," or something similar, it is often ignored. It is expected! *Of course the pastor would say that,* the counselee is thinking.

When we ask a counselee to observe his family, and make a list of things that are worth continuing, our initial aim will be to clarify these *exceptions to the problem* and find out how they are happening. How are these things happening? What capabilities does the counselee have that he may not be aware of? How can he continue to have these things happen and to build on them? What strengths does he have that helped these exceptions to the problem happen? Quite often the counselee does not realize the significance of these resources.

I have discovered that the problem does not need to be clearly defined for effective counseling to take place. Quite often it *cannot* be clearly defined. Rather, it is the solution that needs to be clearly defined. I would rather ask what is different about the times when this problem does not occur. I am looking for evidence that the Spirit has already placed in the counselee's life: *clues to ways of getting unstuck.*

We can also encourage the counselee to consider what will be different when his problem has been solved, thus altering his focus. As he shifts paradigms from a past focus to a future focus, he will begin to move in a forward direction. Thus, even as he describes what he will be doing differently when the problem is solved, the paradigm is shifting to a solution, or outcome, focus. The counselor assumes that something will be different, thereby suggesting change.

I recall a family who came to see me a couple of years ago. Mom and Dad came in along with their two sons, Jimmy, age ten, and Jonathan, age fourteen. Jimmy had been identified by the rest of the family as the source of most of the problems in the home. They wanted to discuss *his* problems at length. During the course of the counseling session I watched Jimmy become more withdrawn as accusations piled up.

When I helped this family to consider the times when these problems did not happen, they began listing many things that they were quite pleased with and areas in which Jimmy was doing quite well. As the conversation shifted into this more positive approach, I observed him perk up and enter again into the family conversation. I then asked what was different about these times. What was different about Mom and Dad during these times? What was big brother doing differently during these times? What would Jimmy be doing when the family was solving this problem? Was it similar to the things that he was doing that the family identified as working?

The deficiency talk had been ineffective. The solution talk began to move the family toward very interesting exceptions that suggested possibilities for creating solutions. What was exciting is that these strengths and grace events flowed out of the life experience that God had already placed within this family.

3. FINDING EXCEPTIONS HELPS CREATE SOLUTIONS

As you can see in the previous illustrations, in every problem that a family or an individual may be going through there will be some instances in which exceptions occur. These instances represent times when the problem is not happening. They offer clues to solutions that may be created (de Shazer, 1988, pp. 131–51). Unfortunately, these exceptions are not always viewed as important by the counselee. It is the counselor's task to help bring meaning to them. Focusing on these exceptions helps the counselee obtain a new perception, while it is also drawing upon the creative work of the Spirit as He continues the process of maturation.

For example, one married couple who came to see me believed they had done all they could to solve their marital problems. So far nothing had helped, and they were going to try one last time. They wanted to work things out, but the more they talked about it, the more frustrated and angry they became. They still harbored resentment for a number of arguments in the past, usually because of poor communication and a mutual lack of respect. Their efforts often led to confrontations over who was to blame.

After listening carefully to what they had to say and to what they had tried to do to resolve their problems, I complimented them on their sincere efforts. I asked them if there were times when they were not fighting or blaming one another. They looked at each other for a moment and briefly smiled. It turns out that just the week before they had gone out on a "date." They had a nice dinner and went to a movie. They told me it had been a long time since they had "gotten away from it all," so they called it a date. Their children were all at friends' homes for the evening.

Neither saw this date as meaningful but rather as simply a break from their problems. When they went back to discussing their problems the next day, the "break" was over and the arguing began once again. I asked them what was different about their date that caused it to be an enjoyable time. They told me they had agreed not to talk about their problems during the evening. Because of this they were more relaxed with each other.

To me this was quite significant. From my perspective their evening out revealed their ability to communicate; it demonstrated their respect for each other, and it exhibited their capacity to change their problem focus by mutual agreement. I congratulated them on their accomplishment and asked whether this had been a more relaxing and pleasant time for them. They said it was. We considered together how they had been able to create this time with each other, clarifying the strengths that were represented. I wondered if it would be helpful if they spent more time together when they would treat each other as they had on their "date." They said it would be. This became the goal of counseling.

This couple had a paradigm that demanded deficiency communication. According to this paradigm, the only real solution for them was to meet their problems head-on. Unfortunately, it had never worked. Nevertheless, they continued to try the same approach again and again. To me, their "date" was meaningful and revealed within it the couple's real strengths. We had discovered a small portion of the Spirit's writing, but utilizing it required a shift in focus.

In this fashion, exceptions to every problem can be developed jointly by counselor and counselee, and these can be used to develop a solution. As the church counselor continues to clarify these exceptions, the initial goal for the interview begins to take shape.

The counselee will also begin to enjoy a renewed sense of personal control over what had been perceived as a situation that was out of control. I believe these exceptions represent the writing of God's Spirit, pointing to the inner capabilities that He has placed within the counselee. As always God is true to His word and has provided a means of escape (1 Cor. 10:13).

4. THE COUNSELEE IS ALWAYS CHANGING

Conversation that focuses on the problem as the basis for the solution can result in both counselor and counselee becoming overwhelmed with information about past and present problems, as well as future anxieties. Depressed individuals tend to get more depressed when they discuss all the events in their lives that are discouraging them. Anxious people get more anxious. Real change seems further away than ever.

It is interesting to note that most cases of psychiatric care deal with depression. Seventy-five percent of all hospitalizations are due to depression, and only one in fifty depressed individuals who are in counseling are being admitted. Along with this, anxiety is presented as the primary problem in 20–25 percent of all of the rest of professional counseling (Seligman, 1991, p. 79). Depression and anxiety, along with family and marriage problems, will make up the bulk of all counseling, both professional and pastoral.

Unhappiness and fear are areas that ministers and other Christian leaders are quite familiar with and are most prepared to assist. But professional therapists' use of labeling, psychopathologizing, and focusing on problems often leads the church counselor to feel out of his depth. He may come to believe there is nothing that a nonprofessional can do to help a counselee to change.

Yet change is inevitable. Heraclitus is credited with the saying, "It is not possible to place your foot in the same stream twice." As the water is always in motion, so also change in our lives is constantly occurring. If, as a counselor, you conduct your sessions with the expectation that change will occur for the counselees, you will influence them in a positive fashion. Such counselors focus on *change talk*. With a solution-focused approach it is more helpful to think *how* the change will occur, rather than *when* it will occur.

The church counselor knows that God is always doing a new thing. He is going to bring about change in our lives and move us in a direction that accords with His perfect plan. He will use our weaknesses to demonstrate His strength. Of all counselors, the pastor should be a "change talk" counselor.

Small change often leads to bigger change. Jesus taught us to be faithful with the small things in our lives (Matt. 25:21). From the perspective of SFPC it is the small change that begins to make a difference in the counselee's life and becomes the first step toward the solution.

Using words such as "enmeshment" and "dysfunction" are not very helpful. As mentioned earlier, even the recovery movement tends to get locked into a static position when the participant is required to state again and again, "I am an alcoholic." This may be helpful for gaining initial recognition of the seriousness of the problem and for marshaling supportive relationships, but it is based on the disease model of alcoholism. It unwittingly locks the participant into a perception of reality that keeps him victimized and disempowered.

A family may be *acting* in a dysfunctional, enmeshed, or disengaged way, but it is also always changing. When the family focuses on change and solution, the result is the natural transformation that the Holy Spirit has promised. Lock the family or individual into a dysfunctional label, and the avenue for change is greatly minimized.

When are the times the family did not act in a dysfunctional fashion? The alcoholic, gambler, overeater, etc., was not always caught in this cycle of addiction. *What was different about those times*? The counselee is not unalterable. He is going to change. The question is, in what direction is he going?

The Chinese have an interesting word for crisis. It is the word *weichi*. *Wei* means danger, and *chi* means opportunity. Change is inevitable and often results in crisis. A crisis is the breakdown of possibilities. Emotional myopia has blinded the counselee to alternatives that may be readily visible to someone outside of the problem. Yet in the midst of change there is both danger *and* opportunity. *It is the church counselor's task to locate and utilize the opportunity side.*

Is the counselee depressed or is he acting in a depressed fashion? One counselor suggests changing the label into a verb, giving the counselee both responsibility and a measure of control. Thus the counselee would be *depressing* (Glasser, 1984). What is he doing when he is acting in a nondepressed fashion? What is different about those times? Can we pinpoint exceptions to those occasions? If he cannot recall a time when he was not depressed, what will he be doing differently when he is feeling better?

Change is occurring all the time. The counselor is inviting the counselee to seize the opportunity to change in a way that leads toward solution, rather then toward a continuation of the problem.

5. THE COUNSELEE IS THE EXPERT AND DEFINES GOALS

When the counselor is viewed as, or views himself as, an expert on mental disorders, he may guide the counselee toward goals that do not represent the reason for seeking help. Indeed, some counselees want an expert to make the decisions for them. Those who accept this direction may put aside the reason they came for counseling and focus instead on what the expert has proposed.

Often this new goal remains vague because it was not clearly defined in the mind of the counselee. He may not work as hard at achieving it since there is no ownership of the goal. Where should the responsibility for goals and progress be placed?

> [Many] therapy models ... utilize the therapist as the expert in determining what is wrong (diagnosis) and setting the course of treatment. This role and process are similar to those of the physician who makes an observation and conducts tests concerning the symptoms, and then as the expert in pathology and treatment prescribes a course of treatment for the patient. The solution-focused model places responsibility on the other side of the relationship ... clients are the experts on what they want to change, as well as in determining what they want to work on.
>
> *Walter & Peller, 1992, p. 28*

When we acknowledge the counselee as the expert, we are recognizing the resourcefulness that proceeds from his own personal history and grace events. Consider the story of Edward Nelson. When he entered my office, he was uncomfortable, not knowing how to begin. He and his wife, Terri, were members of a local church, and Ed had come to me for help. After talking a while about general things, I asked him what his goal was in coming to see me. This seemed to help him focus his thinking.

"Terri and I have been having some difficulties. I've been looking around for a counselor in town that we could afford. I made a number of inquiries, and we finally found a psychologist over at the Psychological Services Counseling Center. We needed some help with my son from my first marriage. His mom has had trouble dealing with him now that he's a teenager, and she wants me to take custody. Terri and I have a daughter of our own who is four years old. This has become a conflict for us, and it seems to be focused on my son."

I nodded thoughtfully and encouraged him to go on.

"We've been going to this psychologist for the last four weeks. Actually I only went once; he requested to see Terri alone after the first session. I guess he figured she needed more help in dealing with some of her own problems. Terri is not a very confident person, even though she has been very successful at work. I mean, I'd be the first to admit that there are some problems. I sometimes have problems with my anger."

"How have you been able to deal with this?" I asked.

"Not so well, I'm afraid," Ed continued. "We had a big blowup over my son. We got real loud and we pushed each other. This wasn't even over such a big problem. It was a stupid fight. I'm not making any excuses; I just don't want to lose Terri."

"So, how has the counseling been progressing?" I asked.

"In the first session," Ed replied, "the therapist said that Terri was an emotionally battered wife. I was shocked when he said it, but I guess I have been pretty stupid at times. He also suggested I enter into therapy on my own since in his view I'm a spouse abuser. Now Terri is reading books on being an abused wife and is seeing the therapist alone.

"I feel left out, and I don't know what to do. Terri had wanted us to get into counseling for a long time, and I always said no. I just didn't want to discuss our problems with a stranger. When I finally agreed to go, I was the one who found the psychologist and made the appointment. I was proud of myself that I had been able to do this. Now I'm being asked not to attend. He also said he won't see us together due to confidentiality, since he is now Terri's therapist."

"Well, I can't change Terri—or this therapist," I carefully responded. "I do understand that you're not pleased with the way things are progressing. Is there something else I can help you with?"

"Well, it's gotten worse," Ed responded. "Now Terri is saying that she doesn't love me anymore. She's considering moving out with our daughter. She says she needs to take control of her life and has even placed a deposit on an apartment. I guess I haven't been attentive enough. We had a fight over this too, but we made up the next morning and everything seemed to be okay."

"I'm so sorry to hear that," I answered. "I find it interesting that you were able to make up the next morning. What was different about that?"

Ed went on to describe a number of differences that we could have explored for creating an initial goal for marital counseling, but I did not think his primary goal had been addressed yet.

"Let's step out on faith and say that this session has been helpful to you," I said. "How will you know it has been helpful?"

"Well, I guess I would have received another opinion, and some help in figuring out what to do next."

Ed's goal for seeing me was for help in figuring out what to do now that his wife was attending sessions alone. I could have moved in an entirely different direction if I had insisted on my expertise over his. It is possible that the other counselor had done that very thing, but it was too early to tell. Even if he had, it was not something I could change.

"Hmm, when you made the appointment, what was your reason again?" I asked, seeking clarification.

"I wanted help in working with my son," Ed replied. "I guess the psychologist saw something he thought was more important. Perhaps

Terri wanted to talk about her feelings too. I'm out of the picture now. We haven't talked about my son at all, or our marriage. I don't think Terri is really satisfied either. I believe she really wanted to work on our marriage, but it's getting harder to do that now. He keeps asking her how she feels about everything, and my wife is a take-charge kind of person. She wants to see some progress. The counseling doesn't seem to be going anywhere."

At this point we took a break. When I returned I congratulated Ed for his resolve in finding a counselor, as well as his openness and honesty with me. I briefly discussed how therapists approach counseling differently with presuppositions that guide their approach to counseling. I explained that my approach is to focus on solutions rather than on problems. I asked him to observe his marriage and take note of the things that he would like to continue to have happen. I then made myself available to him and Terri in case they wanted to see me together.

There is clear evidence that when the counselee chooses the goal, and works on it together with the counselor, he is more likely to succeed (Miller, 1995). Ed and Terri did come back together to see me. First we worked on their goal regarding Ed's son, and this eventually led into discussion and progress regarding their marriage. When they realized that it was up to them to be fully involved in the process of counseling, they became committed to the goals they themselves had set.

Often a counselee will approach an interview with a whole "laundry list" of problems that he wishes to discuss. After listening carefully, the counselor will need to ask quite specifically what his goal is. Usually, the counselee will have a goal, even if only a vague one. It may be a general statement such as "I want to be happy again" or "I don't want to be depressed." Then the church counselor can begin to help the counselee clarify and describe this initial goal, rather than pursuing a goal that does not come out of the counselee's own reason for seeking help originally.

Matthew Selekman mentions a nationwide poll that the *American Health* magazine conducted to analyze how people solved their problems.

> The vast majority of the people interviewed indicated that they are ten times more likely to change on their own without the help of doctors, therapists and self-help groups. . . . One of the most surprising findings was that only three percent of the time did doctors help these people change whereas psychologists, psychiatrists and

> self-help groups got even less credit for personal changes. Family and close friends were ranked as providing the most support in helping with change.
>
> *Selekman, 1993, p. 33*

6. SOLUTIONS ARE COCREATED

Every person seeks to understand, evaluate, and assimilate individual experiences and information. This process can prevent us from noticing and utilizing new evidence. Keep in mind that meaning is perception. Let us reconsider the story of the three people who witnessed the man raising his hand in front of a small child.

Remember that one reported he saw a man preparing to strike a child. The next said he saw the man waving to someone. The third said the man was simply stretching. Each had infused meaning into the event by his own perception of the situation. Perhaps all three were wrong. Each was limited by his perception, which in turn created "reality" for him. Yet if each refused to admit to the possibility that his perception was incorrect, or unhealthy, then his perception may prevent him from noticing and using information that would allow him to see an alternate possibility. In other words, the observers are stuck in their perception.

So then, all of us are creating our own reality that in turn takes hold of who we are. As church counselors, our task is to cocreate with the counselee a reality in which there is an opportunity for positive change. We can do this by recognizing the writing of the Spirit in his past or present situation, or through cocreating a future in which the problem does not dominate. We minister through what God has already been doing and seek to move the counselee forward toward his goal.

We begin by revealing differences in the way the counselee has perceived his problem—to introduce an alternate perception. "A change in meaning is a change in experience" (Walter & Peller, 1992, p. 26). That is, any change in how the counselee perceives the problem may result in a reevaluation of the experience of that problem. Experience has been altered through the change in meaning.

At one time a woman who came to see me was concerned about a dream she had. In it she saw herself leaving her body and viewing her entire life, from birth to the present moment. But what she saw isolated only the tragic events in her life. Child abuse, trauma, confusion, an emotionally draining marriage. The dream was so powerful that she could not remove herself from its influence. She believed it might represent her death, and she longed to get through the season of the year that the dream represented.

Believing the dream to have greater significance than ordinary dreams, she thought it may have come from God. Even though the dream had no "true" reality, it was still having a powerful influence on her life. She was losing sleep and had become quite unhappy. I offered an alternate perception. Since God is a God of love and His plan for our lives is good, I wondered if the dream might rather represent the Spirit taking all the tragic moments of her life and externalizing them. In this way her problems were placed outside of herself and she was free to live without their negative influence.

I then inquired what would be different for her today if this was the case. She began to describe what would be different if the devastating events really were separated from her present life. She depicted a life much more pleasing and satisfying. The rest of our time was spent clarifying this "vision" of her life without the problem. Carefully and deliberately we cocreated an initial view of this future, which in turn helped her to get on track toward this goal.

It's interesting that there never was an actual, physical experience but rather a highly disturbing dream that triggered past memories. Nevertheless, this dream, which had no "true" existence, had a profound effect on her life. *Her perception of the dream had given birth to meaning. The meaning gave birth to experience. Although there never was a "true" experience, it was experience all the same.* To try to convince her otherwise would have been counterproductive. It was real to her and was now forming her in a negative way. Did God have an intention for this experience? By faith I say yes (see Rom. 8:28).

I also believe His intention is to create faith and hope in the future. "'For I know the plans I have for you,' declares the LORD, 'plans to prosper you and not to harm you, plans to give you hope and a future'" (Jer. 29:11). The possibility I offered, though not provable in an absolute sense, was in keeping with the revealed intention God has for us. This change of perception changed the meaning, transforming the experience.

As counselors we walk hand in hand with the counselee. We "rejoice with those who rejoice, and mourn with those who mourn" (Rom. 12:15). As we work with the counselee, we enter into what he is experiencing. Then we cocreate with him a solution that is more in keeping with faith in God's past preparation and with hope in the future that the Spirit is leading us to.

7. THE COUNSELEE IS NOT THE PROBLEM, THE PROBLEM IS

Psychopathology implies that personal problems are associated with mental diseases; e.g., the counselee *is* obsessive-compulsive, rather than the counselee is *acting* in an obsessive-compulsive fashion. The individual thus labeled may be unable to envision himself as having the ability to change. In SFPC problems do not necessarily indicate psychopathology.

> Problems occur in the context of human interaction and, usually, problems "just happen." Problem patterns include both behavior and perceptions. Both behaving differently and thinking differently are part of the process of change. It is more helpful to consider, "what gets in the way of the client's finding or noticing solutions?", than "what causes this problem?"
>
> *Durrant, 1993, p. 12*

Saying problems "just happen" is not to deny human culpability nor the free will God has given us. Nor should it ignore the consequences of sin. Rather, the context is usually that of a counselee who is trying quite hard to solve his problem; making the decision to come to a counselor reveals the intensity of his desire for change. But what he is doing so far has not been effective. Then, as most of us do at times, he does even more of what has not been working. He focuses on the problem and fails to see potential solutions.

Carl is a thirty-three-year-old man from a local church; he came to see me after seeing a psychiatrist. His family had set up the psychiatric visit, but he wanted to talk to a pastor. His minister referred him to me. He had been diagnosed as being obsessive-compulsive and was feeling discouraged.

The doctor had prescribed an antidepressant and referred him to a therapist who was expert in systematic behavioral treatment. The diagnosis and medication worried him, and this was the reason for his visit with me.

Carl maintained numerous rituals in order to support himself in regard to his interpersonal relationships. What had started as a helpful habit had become a burden. Now his compulsions were seriously hindering his relationship with his fiancée. He knew these rituals had gotten out of hand, but when he tried to interrupt them, the ensuing anxiety was unbearable. I listened as he explained not only his rituals but also his concerns regarding *being* obsessive-compulsive. He continued taking his medication as it offered him some relief and made him better able to make use of our time together. But this label had already served to lock him into the problem.

Although the DSM–4 designation was useful as a descriptive term, I did not believe it was helping therapeutically, so I *reframed* the problem, saying, "It's your habits pushing you around." During the interview we looked for times that his habits did not "push him around." These exceptions then became the focus of counseling. It turned out that there were plenty of such occasions, but he had not viewed them as significant. We continued to focus on exceptions to the problem, finding clues to the writing of the Spirit.

The initial goal had been to do more of what was working and to *observe* what was happening. *This began the process of changing his focus from his being the problem to the habits being the problem.* Each time I used a tracking scale (see chap. 11) to help visualize his progress. A 10 represented life without being beaten up by these fears, and a 1 represented how he was when we started. At the beginning of each session he reported movement up the scale. How he did so became the focus of that session.

After we met together four times, with two follow-up sessions six months later, he was focusing more on what he was doing when he was not being controlled by these habits. His "compulsions" were becoming less frequent and his *competency* and *confidence* were increasing. What had been labeled as a mental disorder was primarily an unsuccessful attempt to resolve difficulties (Watzlawick et al., 1974). Under his psychiatrist's supervision, the medication was decreased and finally dispensed with. Carl's despondency lifted as his capabilities increased.

If a counselee continues to view a problem situation in a certain way, it becomes increasingly difficult for him to gain a new perception. It is more useful to encourage the counselee to avoid doing "more of the same" (Watzlawick et al., 1974). Yet we live in a society where we are quite accustomed to going to experts to get help with any number of situations that we might face in life. In this case going to an expert counselor who views the counselee through the lens of psychopathology and whose paradigm results in deficiency language may result in the counselee's gaining "insight" that is actually a projection from the expert. It may not be valid for the counselee; however, once the diagnosis is accepted as true, he often acts accordingly, sometimes actually defending the label as a part of his identity.

This issue is especially prevalent in marital counseling. In this context it is the spouses who tend to view each other as the problem. Using labels such as dysfunctional, codependent, and emotionally dependent tend to turn the focus on one or both persons *as the problem.* Once again the problem has become squarely focused in a person. Of course, both parties are more than ready to enter into this approach: "If my husband would only. . . ." "If my wife would only. . . ." It is the expectation of focusing on the problem that prevents many couples from seeking help: "We're just going to rehash all our problems with a stranger, and I don't need that."

In the vast majority of cases the primary problem is the way both parties are *interacting*. My standard comment to such couples is, "*You* are not the problem, and *you* are not the problem; your interaction is the problem." This frees both parties from viewing each other as the problem and makes them a team in dealing with a common problem—the *interaction*. Change the *interaction* in a deliberate way, jointly agreed upon, and the couple is on the way to a potential solution—a far more satisfying outcome.

When this occurs the counselee no longer views himself or another person *as the problem*, rather the *problem* is the problem. Instead of being disempowered, he has become empowered, creating a potential for rapid improvement. From a pastoral perspective, this is in keeping with *intentionality*. God's Spirit has brought about a new creation in Christ. As counselors we wish to help the counselee proceed forward into it.

8. THE COUNSELING RELATIONSHIP IS POSITIONAL

The psychotherapeutic idea of *resistance* is not a useful concept. *It implies that the client does not want to change* and is based on the dynamics of power and control in the counseling session. It is far more helpful to assume that the counselee wants something to change but may not perceive the change as within his control.

In one solution-focused approach the counselee is viewed as either a customer, a complainant, or a visitor (de Shazer, 1988, p. 42). These distinctions are not viewed as fixed characteristics. Rather, they are used as guidelines for describing *positions*, or possible positions, that the client may take during the counseling session. These positions are often a reaction to the perceived positions of the counselor. Like detectives we are alert to listen for indications of the counselee's position so as to identify his immediate level of cooperation regarding the counseling relationship.

Although I agree with this approach, I prefer different terms. As nouns they can imply a fixed state. I have observed them used in this fashion by clinicians as well. For example, the counselee can be viewed *as* a complainant and so be unintentionally labeled. A result may be that the counselor responds to the counselee as being in that fixed state. This counters the intention of the designations.

I choose to make the terms grammatically descriptive. In this way they depict how a counselee is behaving *at the moment*. I have also used language that church counselors will be more at home with. Therefore, a customer is someone who is in a *willing position*; a complainant is someone who is in a *blaming position*; and, a visitor is someone who is in an *attending position.*

Question: So, how many therapists does it take to screw in a light bulb? Answer: Just one . . . but the light bulb has to be willing. It is an old joke, but one that seems fitting to the situation. Being willing is also the most important prerequisite to spiritual growth.

A counselee who is in a *willing* position is one who enters the interview with a clear problem. It could be about someone else or about himself. It is possible in the initial conversation to get a clear picture of the situation and understand that the counselee is ready to do something about it. As the description implies, the counselee is willing to try doing something different because what he is presently doing is not working. He wants to work with the counselor to resolve the problem. Appraising willingness, as well as looking for clues to exceptions, is a primary task of the "attentive listening" portion of the interview.

A counselee who is in a *blaming* position is one who comes to the interview with a great deal of information about a problem someone else has. This person does not see himself as part of the solution. A wife may come in to see the pastor with a problem regarding her husband or child. The person in a blaming position knows a great deal about the situation and can help the counselor better understand it. But *he wants the other person to be different*. The other person is defined as the problem. The counselee views himself as waiting helplessly for this person to change. He is convinced that the other person must change before the relationship can change.

By contrast, the counselee may see himself as a victim of his situation or his past. He may have come to believe, perhaps having been told by another counselor or the media, that he has a psychiatric disorder or disease. Either way, the solution is viewed as outside of himself. He does not perceive himself as capable of achieving a positive outcome.

A counselee who is in an *attending* position is one who comes to the interview unwillingly. This could be a spouse who dutifully comes to counseling to please his or her partner. Or it could be a child seeing a counselor because of the parents' or teacher's wishes. On rare occasions it could be someone whom the court ordered into therapy, with the court approving a church counselor to do the counseling. Either way, it is not the counselee's intention to be in counseling. He is there because someone else wants him there. He is uncommitted and often uninvolved in therapy. Others may see him as needing counseling, but he has no goal or agenda to discuss with the counselor.

Again, these distinctions are not viewed as fixed characteristics. They are guidelines for describing positions or possible positions the client may take during the counseling session in relationship to the perceived attitude of the counselor. They represent the counselee's *level of cooperation* regarding the counseling relationship. SFPC seeks to discover ways that encourage the counselee to become a *willing* participant in the counseling process. This is accomplished by coming alongside the counselee's goals, at whatever level of cooperation he may be able to offer.

For example, Johnny, age fourteen, was brought in to see me by his parents. In the initial interview he sat quietly as Mom and Dad described the aspects of his behavior that they were not pleased with. At this juncture the parents were in a *blaming* position and Johnny was simply *attending*. When I saw Johnny alone, I asked him what his reason was for seeing me.

"My Mom and Dad made me come," he said.

"What do you think are your parents' reasons for wanting us to talk together?" I wondered. Johnny gave some of the obvious reasons; he had heard them again and again. Picking up on his *attending* position, as well as doing a little "subliminal seeding" I asked, "I know the Bible says to honor your father and your mother, but sometimes it's real hard isn't it?" Johnny simply smiled in agreement.

"It must be a pain having your parents on your back all the time," I said. "Would you like me to try to get them off your back?"

"Sure, but how?" was Johnny's simple reply. He has also now moved momentarily into a more *willing* position, since we were talking about something that concerned him.

"Well, one way to get your parents off your back is to prove them wrong, like showing them you are not such a problem all the time and taking some responsible steps to turn this thing around. Can you think of some steps you could take to prove your parents wrong about you?"

As Johnny began to describe some of the things he could do, he started to develop a workable goal that he could take ownership of. His task would be to do a little of this and see what happens. Afterward, when I spoke to his parents privately, I asked them to look for changes in Johnny's attitude or behaviors in the coming week. Look for the things he is doing that you would like him to continue to do. Mom and Dad said they were *willing* to do this simple goal. Johnny's parents are now actively looking for his good aspects (no matter how deeply hidden!) at the same time that Johnny is going to be trying to "prove them wrong." Both parents and teen are now in a *willing* position regarding these simple, initial counseling goals.

9. THE COUNSELOR'S FOCUS IS ON SOLUTIONS

There are three rules that have been formulated to help a counselor stay more focused on solutions. They can be stated in this fashion:

> Rule one: "If it's not broken, don't fix it!"
>
> Rule two: "Once you know what works, do more of it!"
>
> Rule three: "If it doesn't work, don't do it again. Do something different!"

I have found these rules helpful and actually quite profound. They pass the "common sense test." Many people live this way without realizing it, but they do not see their behavior as meaningful. When used as a way to stay focused in the counseling interview, these rules are highly beneficial. But they need not be viewed as rules—rather, they are guidelines that inform the counseling relationship. They are assumptions that influence the way the *counselor thinks* about counseling.

The first guideline simply reminds the counselor to find out what the counselee wants. The church counselor can fall into the same trap that many professional therapists fall into—that is, seeing himself as an expert. The counselee has come for help. That puts the counselor into an expert position. This is not a helpful position to be in. No matter how much theological or psychological training a counselor may have had, he is not an expert on the counselee. As we have said before, each counselee is unique, and only God knows the whole story about him.

The counselor who operates from an expert approach tends to get into situations that require greater and greater use of personal experience. He is forced to rely on his own personal constructs, i.e., the way *he* makes sense of life, viewing the counselee through his own lens, his own perceptions. For example, pastors are accustomed to having a certain amount of freedom in telling people what they should do, but this is not always necessary to counsel effectively. Yet the counselee is often willing to be led by an expert. Our culture has prepared him for this attitude. It also puts the burden of responsibility on the expert to fix the problem.

But when the counselor's admonitions or assignments miss the mark, it is because they have not proceeded from the counselee's goal for seeking counsel. The "expert" may blame the counselee for any lack of success in the counseling. He is resistant, or he is holding on to a sinful lifestyle. He is not ready to get serious with God. However, the counselee may blame the "expert." He may think to himself, *If he were a better counselor I would not still be having all these problems.* Not only is this approach not helpful for the counselee, it is also very fatiguing to the counselor.

What is the counselee's goal in coming for counseling? How can this goal be utilized to create a solution? Often, the counselee comes into the counseling interview telling us what he *does not want.* He has become so problem-focused that he only knows he wants the pain or frustration to stop. The task of SFPC is to help the counselee define what he *does want* and then help "craft" that goal into a workable solution. This will not happen if the counselor's personal intentions override the counselee's goals.

The second guideline, "Once you know what works, do more of it," seems apparent. Look for what God has already placed into the counselee's life that is working and do more of that. Yet, even though the Bible teaches us to look to God for our strength, much of our training has prepared us to look for what is wrong. We tell ourselves that when we find out what the problem is, we can begin to fix it. *The difficulty is that you can rarely get two people to agree on what the problem is!* This is one of the most frustrating aspects of family or marital counseling when the methodology is problem-focused.

We need to specifically train ourselves to look for what is right, what is working for the counselee. Once an exception to the problem is discovered, the goal of counseling is more readily clarified. The basic assumption is that if it's not working, you should stop doing it. If it is working, you should do more of it.

The third guideline, "If it doesn't work, don't do it again. Do something different," is the opposite of the old adage "If at first you don't succeed, try, try again." We have grown up on stories that teach persistence and tenacity—good qualities indeed, but not in the face of methods that are not working. It is the counselee's own paradigm that blinds him to other options.

I am reminded of a mother who came with her thirteen-year-old daughter to another solution-focused counselor. The relationship between mother and daughteer was suffering, and the mother did not know what else to do. When they fought, it usually ended in a physical altercation. During the course of the counseling interview the mother was asked if what she was doing was working. She said it was not, but in desperation she wondered what else she could do. The counselor suggested doing something different, anything different. In keeping with this advice, this mom came upon the idea of dancing whenever she was getting ready to begin yelling. Where this idea originated is anyone's guess, but since it was her idea, it was worth trying.

As it turned out, this so surprised her daughter that it interrupted the *pattern* that was leading to the terrible fights. Mom was no longer "dancing the fight dance" with her daughter—she was actually dancing! Therefore, her daughter had no one to fight with. This gave room for the Spirit to intervene, and it opened the door for more constructive solutions in counseling. Her daughter thought mom had "gone crazy," but she was smiling when she said it.

SUMMARY

Here again, with brief summary statements, are the nine assumptions that help form the attitudes that solution-focused church counselors have regarding the counseling process:

1. God Is Already Active in the Counselee

This truth is vital in determining whether we, as church counselors, are going to trust what God has already been doing in the counselee. When we do, we begin to look for clues, e.g., the writing of the Spirit, grace events, strengths, exceptions to the problem—all to discover how God has already been guiding and preparing him. There are capabilities within the counselee that God has already revealed in his past that will help him effectively manage a specific problem in a way that is pleasing to God. We look for these clues and build upon them, rather than focusing on the problems.

2. Complex Problems Do Not Demand Complex Solutions

No matter what the problem may be that is bringing individuals into counseling, that problem does not happen all the time. There are good times, times in their lives when they are happy. The problem does not need to be clearly defined for effective counseling to take place.

Quite often it cannot be clearly defined. Rather, it is the solution that needs to be clearly defined. I would rather ask what is different about the times when this problem does not occur. I am looking for evidence the Spirit has already placed in the counselee's life—clues to ways of getting unstuck.

3. Finding Exceptions Helps Create Solutions

Finding the writing of the Spirit demands a shift in paradigms from a problem focus to a solution focus. Exceptions to every problem can be developed by the counselor and counselee, and these can be used to develop goals and outcomes. These exceptions to the problem need to be clarified; they form the initial goal for counseling. They represent God's finger pointing to the inner capabilities that He has placed within the counselee.

4. The Counselee Is Always Changing

Change in our lives is a constant occurrence. The counselor conducts the session expecting change to occur and focusing on change talk. It is more helpful to think about *when* the change will occur rather than *if* it will occur. Small change often leads to bigger change.

5. The Counselee Is the Expert and Defines Goals

When the counselee chooses the goal and works on it together with the counselor, he is more likely to succeed. When we acknowledge the counselee as the expert, we are recognizing that there is a resourcefulness that proceeds from his own personal history and grace events. Since we are not specifically looking for the cause of the problem, we can assist the counselee in getting on track toward creative solutions.

6. Solutions Are Cocreated

We each are creating our own reality, which in turn takes hold of who we are. As church counselors, our task is to cocreate with the counselee a reality in which there is an opportunity for positive change. We work through what God has already been doing and seek to move the counselee forward toward his goal.

7. The Counselee Is Not the Problem, the Problem Is

Problems do not indicate psychopathology. Problems occur in the setting of human interaction and, usually, just happen. Both behaving differently and thinking differently are part of the process of change. It is more helpful to consider what gets in the way of finding or noticing solutions than what causes the problem.

8. The Counseling Relationship Is Positional

We describe how a counselee is behaving by using language that depicts the position the counselee is in at the moment. Someone who is in a *willing position* has a clear sense of the problem and is ready to work with the counselor toward solution. Someone who is in a *blaming position* has a great deal of information about the other person but does not see himself as part of the solution. Someone who is in an *attending position* is there because someone else wants him there. He is uncommitted and often uninvolved in therapy. Others may see him as needing counseling but he has no goal or agenda to express to the counselor.

SFPC seeks to discover ways that every counselee can become a *willing* participant in the counseling process. This is accomplished by coming alongside the counselee's goals, at whatever level of cooperation he may be able to offer initially.

9. The Counselor's Focus Is on Solutions

Basic guidelines for staying solution-focused in counseling are these: If it's not broken, don't fix it; once you know what works, do more of it; and if it doesn't work, don't do it again—do something different. These guidelines are used as a way to stay focused in the counseling interview, and they inform the counseling relationship. It is the way the counselor *thinks* about counseling. ■

CHAPTER EIGHT

Personal Integrity: Ethical Guidelines

As a general definition ethical practices benefit the [counselee]; unethical practices are done for the practitioner's benefit. ▪ *Gerald Corey, 1991, p. 56*

Many excellent books have been written regarding ethical practice in counseling.* Of course, ethical considerations are as important to a pastor or Christian leader who is counseling within the local church as they are to the professional therapist, psychologist, or psychiatrist.** It is not my intention to cover ethical issues that have been clearly presented elsewhere. Yet the church counselor needs to have a clear understanding of the ethical concerns that inform his counseling procedures.

---

*One that I recommend is *Sex in the Forbidden Zone,* by Peter Rutter (New York: Fawcett, 1989).

**The following organizations all have ethics committees:

American Association of Pastoral Counselors (AAPC), 9508A Lee Hwy., Fairfax, VA 22031–(703) 385–6967.

American Association for Marriage and Family Therapy (AAMFT), 1717 K St. NW, #407, Washington, DC 20006–(202) 429–1825.

American Psychiatric Association (APA), 1400 K St. NW, Washington, DC 20005–(202) 682–6000.

The ethical guidelines that guide my counseling and that I recommend to those I train are these:

1. Remain alert to your limitations.
2. Counseling must be informed by a theoretical framework of identity formation and therapeutic assumptions.
3. The rights of the counselee are primary.
4. Make every effort to refrain from dual relationships.
5. Be sure the counselee is aware of the responsibilities or limitations of the counseling relationship.
6. The counselor must not become romantically or sexually intimate with a counselee.
7. Do not use diagnostic or treatment procedures that you have not been professionally trained in.

1. REMAIN ALERT TO YOUR LIMITATIONS.

Once again, it is good to remember that when something is not working, you should stop doing it and do something different. Not only is this a basic assumption regarding a solution-focused approach, it is also true regarding the counselee's right to be referred to another counselor when no progress is being made. The American Counseling Association (ACA) states in its code of ethics: "If the counselor determines an inability to be of professional assistance to the [counselee], the counselor must either avoid initiating the counseling relationship or immediately terminate the relationship" (1988).

The American Association of Pastoral Counselors (AAPC) states in its code of ethics: "We do not abandon or neglect clients. If we are unable, or unwilling for appropriate reasons, to provide professional help or continue a professional relationship, every reasonable effort is made to arrange for continuation of treatment with another professional."

A counselor using a solution-focused approach should be tenacious. My experience reveals that focusing on strengths is effective and in harmony with scriptural revelation. Yet a pastor is ethically constrained to refer if counseling remains ineffective. Keep in mind that major problems are rarely solved simply or quickly. Getting counselees on track to solutions is the priority of SFPC. If, after two or three sessions, the church counselor remains unable to encourage the counselee to achieve an outcome-focused *shift in thinking*, it is time to refer.

A pastor or other Christian counselor should be well acquainted with the Christian counseling resources within the community. Professional Christian counseling agencies, peer self-help groups, support groups, crisis intervention services—such as those offered for battered wives or counseling regarding pregnancy, day-treatment programs as well as skill-building workshops—all are helpful as referral or adjunct services.

Every minister and church leader who is engaged in the ministry of counseling should also consider the following:

a. Counselors should have access to qualified supervision.
b. Consultation with fellow pastors and counselors is crucial for maintaining professional accountability. The willingness to reach out for consultation is evidence of professional maturity.
c. Consultation is also vital when one is counseling those who may be potentially suicidal or dangerous to others. I strongly encourage membership in a local pastoral counselors association when possible.
d. It is imperative that suspected physical problems be examined by a physician when indicated. Also, it is good practice for the pastor to maintain a working relationship with a Christian psychiatrist for purposes of consultation regarding counselees who exhibit bizarre behaviors or are deeply depressed.
e. Counselors should be aware of cultural differences and how they may affect the counseling relationship. A counselor may be acting unethically when cultural differences are not considered.

2. COUNSELING MUST BE INFORMED BY A THEORETICAL FRAMEWORK OF IDENTITY FORMATION AND THERAPEUTIC ASSUMPTIONS.

Assumptions guide us in the practice of counseling. The counselor must clearly understand these assumptions, and procedures should flow naturally from them. It is important for the counselor to have a clear methodology that he follows when counseling. Sharing some Scriptures or hoping he will think of something that will be helpful does not qualify as a clear theoretical framework for working with individuals who are in crisis.

Even though the counselee is the expert, the counselor must also be skillful and growing in proficiency in regard to his chosen methodology. He should be improving his skills and knowledge through continuing education, counseling journals, and publications—preferably with a solution-focused emphasis.

3. THE RIGHTS OF THE COUNSELEE ARE PRIMARY.

You cannot give what you do not have. The counselor models spiritual and emotional health. We who are pastors and leaders in the church do not need to be perfect, just honest about our imperfections. When dishonesty, either subtle or obvious, is allowed to take root, the counselor may become more concerned with meeting his own needs than meeting those of the counselee.

This dishonesty will be revealed in counseling through various facets of the counselor's personality. He may manifest any of the following: a need to demonstrate power and control, a need for approval and affection, a need to feel respected and appreciated, a need to feel qualified as a counselor, a need to impose theological positions, a need to be needed, or a need to be nurtured. If the counselor has one or more of the above needs, he seeks to meet them through the counselee. He puts his own needs above the counselee's.

If the counselor is depending, consciously or unconsciously, on the counselee for his own emotional fulfillment, he may try to maintain the counselee in a position of dependence. If he is not able to do so, he may begin to resent the counselee or feel uncomfortable in his presence. It is essential to preserve clear guidelines to focus the counseling dialogue. It is more effective, and probably more loving, to conduct the counseling session professionally—with the counselor being primarily conscious of the counselee's need for empowerment.

4. MAKE EVERY EFFORT TO REFRAIN FROM DUAL RELATIONSHIPS.

It is quite difficult to be attentive to the counseling relationship while at the same time trying to sustain a personal friendship with the counselee. Although most SFPC is brief in nature, it still places the counselor in a position of authority and influence over the counselee. There is always a danger of indirectly misusing this position.

Therefore I always refer family members, elders, deacons, those who work for me, or those with whom I have personal friendships. The reason is simple—counseling changes the relationship. This is not to say that I would not listen to, support, educate, or minister to these individuals. What I avoid is a counseling relationship.

The AAPC states, "We recognize the trust placed in and the unique power of the therapeutic relationship. While acknowledging the complexity of some pastoral relationships, we avoid exploiting the trust and dependency of clients. We avoid those dual relationships with clients (e.g., business or close personal relationships) which could impair our professional judgment, compromise the integrity of the treatment, and/or use the relationship for our own gain."

5. BE SURE THE COUNSELEE IS AWARE OF THE RESPONSIBILITIES OR LIMITATIONS OF THE COUNSELING RELATIONSHIP.

Most professional codes of ethics maintain that the counselee has a right to be given enough information in order to make an intelligent choice about entering into counseling. For example, it is too late—and unethical—to explain to a teen from the church's youth group that you are going to inform her parents that she is pregnant and considering an abortion *after* she has revealed these facts to you.

Of course, not every church counseling session will require disclosure of these responsibilities and limitations. There is a balance between providing too much information and not giving enough. Nevertheless, I have discovered that some kind of "*informed-consent document*" is helpful. In it the counselor can briefly state in quickly read statements the general goals and benefits of counseling, risks involved in counseling, limitations and exceptions to confidentiality, the rights of minors, the counselor's personal qualifications, the counselor's responsibilities to the counselee, the counselee's responsibility to the counseling process, and the services the counselee may expect to receive.

Limitations and exceptions to confidentiality need to be given careful attention. Circumstances surrounding confidentiality are not always easily defined and discretion needs to be demonstrated. In general, professional counselors must break confidentiality when it is apparent that the counselee may do serious injury to others or to himself or herself. Abuse to children and the elderly are required by law to be reported.

General guidelines for confidentiality include the following circumstances:

- When the counselee may injure either himself or others (Do not keep a deadly secret.)
- When the counselor believes that the counselee's behavior is bizarre and that he may require hospitalization
- When the counselor believes a counselee under the age of sixteen has been victimized through rape, incest, child abuse, or some other criminal activity

It is also important for the counselor to remember that he should have no professional communication with family or friends of a counselee without written permission.

Members of the AAPC who charge for their services adhere to the following statement: "We do not disclose client confidences to anyone, except: where mandated by law; to prevent a clear and immediate danger to someone; in the course of a civil, criminal or disciplinary action arising from the counseling where the pastoral counselor is the defendant; for purposes of supervision or consultation; or by previously obtained written permission." When discussing a counselee in consultation or supervision, only first names are used or names are changed.

Although a pastor or Christian leader who is counseling within the local church setting may not be under these legal obligations, he is ethically bound to inform the counselee what his criteria are regarding confidentiality.

6. THE COUNSELOR MUST NOT BECOME ROMANTICALLY OR SEXUALLY INTIMATE WITH A COUNSELEE.

Again, whose needs are being met? Remember that the counselee is in a vulnerable position. Thus any attempt at such intimacy is always an abuse of the position of the power and authority that a counselor has with a counselee. Becoming involved with a former counselee may also be unethical; it is a gray area, yet one that I believe should be avoided.

The AAPC position is to the point for all counselors within the local church setting as well: "All forms of sexual behavior or harassment with clients are unethical, even when a client invites or consents to such behavior or involvement."

7. DO NOT USE DIAGNOSTIC OR TREATMENT PROCEDURES THAT YOU HAVE NOT BEEN PROFESSIONALLY TRAINED IN.

There are many diagnostic tests and assessment tools that are used to assess the counselee. Therefore some professional therapists take social, family, and medical data, using personality tests, assessing physical behavior, and evaluating thought content and mental status—all in order to add to their knowledge of the counselee and his situation. The church counselor should not use such tools unless he has been specifically trained to do so.

Fortunately, SFPC does not depend on gathering information; it is a *treatment* procedure. Although this counseling approach employs pastoral strengths and training, those who use it, or any other approach for that matter, should receive instruction and supervision. The primary challenge for those who follow a solution-oriented methodology is to use all their knowledge and training to help the counselee to become aware of his own expertise. The counselee *is the expert* on his life. Therefore we focus on cocreating solutions and trusting the intention of the Spirit. Today a good portion of my counseling library is unused, since it operates from the problem-focused or disease model of counseling. ■

PART TWO

Practice

CHAPTER NINE

The Counseling Interview: Suggesting a Framework for Change

I do not believe in a fate that falls on men however they act; but I do believe in a fate that falls on them unless they act. ▪ *G. K. Chesterton*

I've learned that about 90 percent of the things that happen to me are good and only about 10 percent are bad. To be happy, I just have to focus on the 90 percent. ▪ *H. Jackson Brown, Jr., 1991, p. 156*

"So in everything, do to others what you would have them do to you, for this sums up the Law and the Prophets." ▪ *Matthew 7:12*

Solution-focused pastoral counselors treat people as competent. This is how all counselors would wish to be treated if roles were reversed. We suggest a change in focus, from problems to solutions, while encouraging forward progress toward specific, mutually-agreed-upon goals. These goals suggest outcomes that are clearly described.

An old Sunday school illustration is easily adapted to describe this approach. Visualize a train on a track. The train engine represents the truth of God's Word and the decisions we make. The middle cabin car depicts the decisions we make and what we believe in—our trust and reliance on this truth. The caboose characterizes our emotional life. The caboose is for the use of the train crew; it is where they live on long trips. So also, our emotions are where "we live." Yet, our emotions change. The caboose will follow along once the engine starts moving forward—but the caboose cannot effectively pull the train. The train moves ahead when trust is focused on God's truth—our decisions being made on the basis of what we believe. Forward motion ceases when trust is placed primarily in emotions rather than truth.

But this train also needs a track and a destination. The track illustrates action by drawing attention to the destination. It also communicates the way to go in order to get there. It displays the potential for step-by-step progress out from beneath the heaviness of personal problems. As the train proceeds down the track, its movement characterizes forward progress in counseling. The destination represents the described outcome for the counselee, where problems no longer dominate.

The flowchart in figure 1 is a conceptual schema, depicting the SFPC process from the perspective of various *tracks*. In my workshops and training I teach this quite specifically. Once learned, it should be used only to give structure to a counselor's personal style. It can be viewed as a map showing various avenues of creating solution-focused conversations. It is developed and offered as a means to staying on track in the counseling interview. The flowchart represents a process-oriented approach to describing how the counseling conversation would "ideally" flow. It breaks down the four key components, or processes, of SFPC. ■

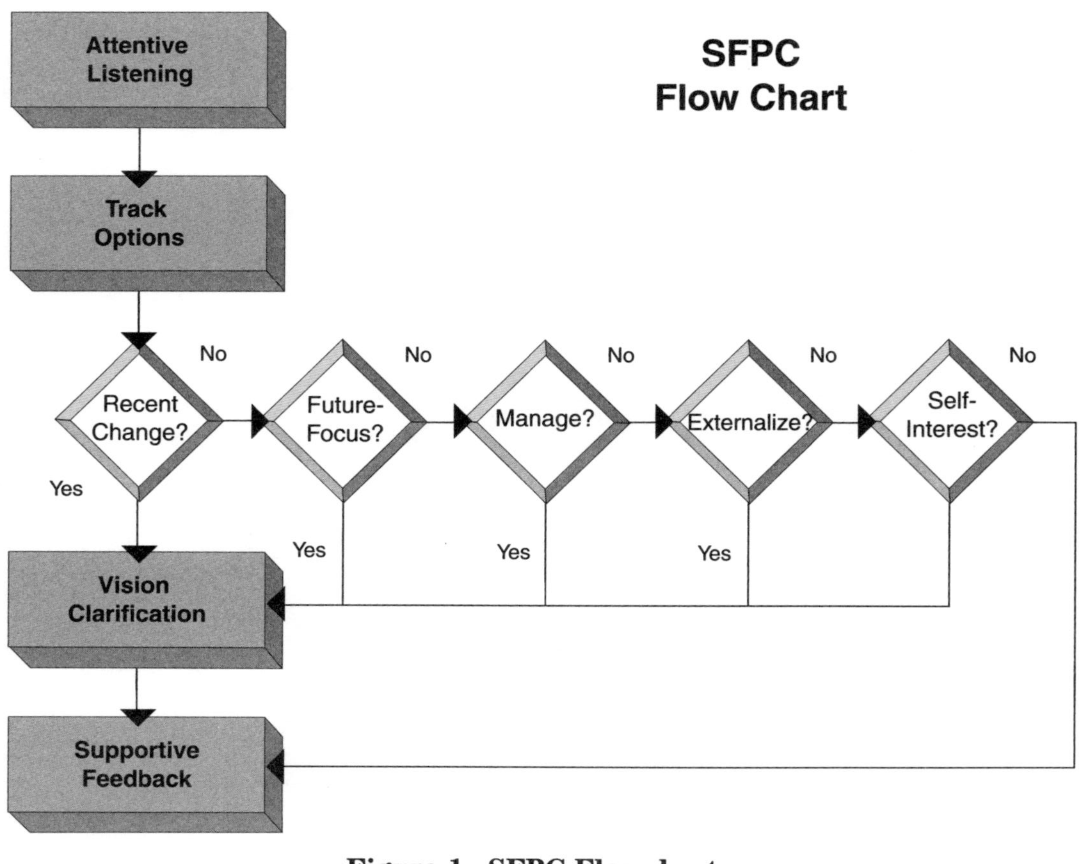

Figure 1. SFPC Flowchart

CHAPTER TEN

Attentive Listening: A Search for Clues

Anything we do in counseling is wasted, if [those who come to us] do not feel that their experience of the situation has been validated. ■ *Michael Durrant, 1993, p.52*

Have you ever had the experience of being in a conversation with an extroverted or distracted individual and realizing that while you are speaking he is already preparing his response, or perhaps only half listening? Often his response has little to do with what you just said. Put two such people together and both are talking, but neither is really listening! Each is responding to his own agenda, regardless of what is being spoken by the other. This is also known as listening *passively*.

Passive listening occurs when the listener is formulating a response while the speaker is still talking. He is only partially listening, leaving the speaker feeling unheard—as if he has wasted his effort in trying to express his thoughts.

Active listening mirrors or paraphrases back to the speaker what he has just said, thus confirming for the speaker that he has been heard. This approach gives the speaker the opportunity to fully express himself. Thus, as in tennis, the ball is constantly hit back into the speaker's court.

Attentive listening is different in intention from both of these approaches. It has the quality of careful, alert listening; that is the ideal of active listening. Yet it is different in purpose. By it the counselor validates feelings while carefully listening for clues that may represent strengths and exceptions. Figure 2 develops this first component of the SFPC flowchart.

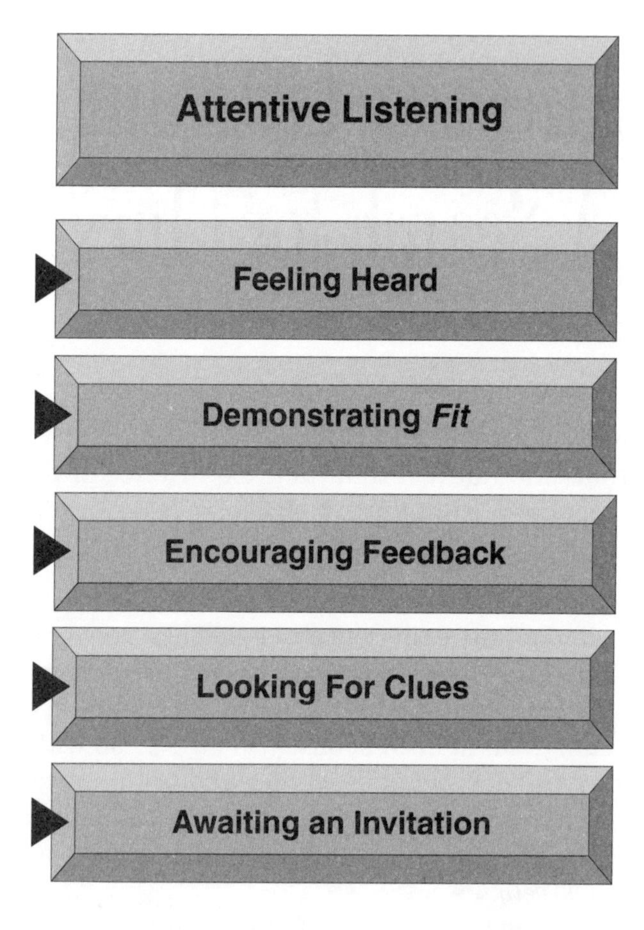

Figure 2. Attentive Listening

The primary emotion attentive listening verifies is the need to have feelings validated. This aspect of attentive listening in the counseling interview should not be overlooked or taken for granted. In a most profound sense it supports the need to feel accepted and heard in a mature, caring relationship.

FEELING HEARD

The intent of SFPC is to establish a collaborative relationship with the counselee. Any help we offer through counseling may be hindered if the counselee does not feel that his experience and understanding of the problem have been heard and appreciated.

Pastoral counseling often concentrates on the cognitive side of counseling, whereas much of secular therapy centers on the affective, i.e., on the feelings and emotions as distinguished from cognition or action. These approaches differ to the extent that acknowledging and expressing emotions are viewed as important to the counseling process. To what degree is the cathartic expression of feelings essential to the process of change? SFPC believes the driving force of change is through the revision of constructs. When the counselee shifts to a solution focus, the process of change begins. Yet the counselor walks a fine line between *hearing* the counselee's feelings of anger or frustration and concentrating primarily on the problem.

I recall the time when a twenty-three-year-old woman came to see me. She was married to a "younger man" of twenty-two and talked nonstop for about fifteen to twenty minutes about how she was "raising" her young husband. She was tired of it. "I just have an older soul," she told me. "He's like a child." In her view he had lied about financial matters, and she was starting to fear he was simply using her to support him. She felt that the differences between them were insurmountable. "He is nothing like what I had expected when we got married. I just want him out!" she said in no uncertain terms. They had been married for seven months!

After seventeen years of marriage and having had training and experience as a pastor and counselor, I had numerous "solutions" to her problems rolling around in my head. Unfortunately, that fact was also evident in my face and through my choice of words. *I was so ready to help her that I was not "listening" to her.* I had too quickly determined that the view she held of her husband's behavior was influencing her responses to him and that her responses were therefore reinforcing his behavior. To a certain extent this determination was accurate, but my desire to help her see this was premature. She did not *feel* heard.

I was offering solutions, but she was in a blaming position; i.e., she perceived the solution to be outside of her control. I needed to respond to her in a way that demonstrated I had really heard her frustration—her feeling of hopelessness. Until I did, she would continue to offer reasons as to why any suggested solution would not work.

I changed gears and began to compliment her on the amount of effort she had put into her marriage up to this point. The fact that she was talking to me showed how seriously she felt about her situation. In her view she seemed to have tried everything, so I praised her for working so hard on her marriage, even though what she had tried had not worked with her husband so far.

I asked her what had prevented their marriage from getting even worse. How had she been able to manage as long as she had? She explained that things were not bad all the time. Here was a clue that might uncover strengths that were waiting to be brought out and given meaning. In this we found an opportunity for constructive collaboration, i.e., fleshing out what was different about these times when things "weren't all bad." She had been heard and had made her first tentative shift from a blaming to a willing position.

DEMONSTRATING *FIT*

In the counseling interview the counselor has the unique opportunity to enter the world of the counselee, and for this, attentive listening is essential. Thus another feature of attentive listening is that it enables the counselor to show that he identifies with and understands the counselee's concerns. Demonstrating this identification is what I mean by *fit*.

"Do two walk together unless they have agreed to do so?" (Amos 3:3). In counseling we want to walk together with the counselee as he proceeds toward solutions. The journey begins in the counseling relationship. What is happening in the session that shows the counselee that the counselor is *with* him? How do we demonstrate this *fit*?

Again, we are to "rejoice with those who rejoice, and mourn with those who mourn" (Rom. 12:15). The counselor needs to demonstrate ways he is *with* the counselee when he is rejoicing (*light emotions*) or mourning (*intense emotions*). His response needs to *fit* the counselee's emotions. It is possible that the counselor may feel compassion while his body language and tone of voice fail to reveal this compassion. When this happens, he is out of agreement. Distance between counselor and counselee is the result, because they are not walking together.

When we are with a counselee, we need to attend to both verbal and nonverbal cues. Our voice should respond to the characteristics of his voice. The inflection and choice of words should reveal understanding. Our physical posture should be similar to his. If the counselee is sitting back, relaxed, with his legs crossed, eventually we should assume a similar position. When he is anxious and concerned, leaning forward, we can join together with him in that position—not exhibiting apprehension but showing that we are "*with him*" in his anxiety.

All the while we should maintain eye contact and focused attention—being totally "*there*" for the counselee. We enter into his problem world long enough to join with him in cocreating a solution, walking together with him out from under the weight of the problem. We are also entering into his hopeful world so that we can more forcefully emphasize the significance of his newly forming hope.

GIVING ENCOURAGING FEEDBACK

It is reported that Mark Twain said he could live for a whole month on one good compliment. I agree. There is power in encouragement. To encourage is to stand alongside another person and place courage into them. I have been blessed with knowing numerous Christians who are loving and supportive people. They have learned that a word of encouragement can go a long way. It is often like a drink of cool water in a dry and thirsty land. A counselee who is in the midst of problems, and often crises, encounters fears and doubts that leave him confused and bewildered. He can benefit greatly from the support, encouragement, and compliments given from someone who stands outside of the problem.

Offering encouragement is certainly in agreement with pastoral intention. Within the counseling interview, encouragement is vital if change is to be reinforced. Counseling, although serious, need not be neutral and solemn. It is more helpful when it is lighthearted. Within the most serious situations, the way out will always include positive emotional support. A cheerful heart is still good medicine (Prov. 17:22).

Encouraging feedback denotes the *posture* that the counselor takes toward the counselee throughout the interview. This posture supports the belief that behavior or thoughts that reflect exceptions to the problem need to be emphasized as significant to the counselee. Even small changes in posture are meaningful when they reveal instances of strengths or exceptions to conflicts.

The counselor is consistently turning the spotlight on *hope* in order to create a more encouraging counseling environment. I sometimes view the word *HOPE* as an acrostic to signify a *Hopeful*, *Optimistic*, *Positive*, and *Expectant* counseling climate. *Webster's Collegiate Dictionary* offers these definitions:

Hopeful: "desire accompanied by expectation of or belief in fulfillment."

Optimistic: "an inclination to put the most favorable construction upon actions and events or to anticipate the best possible outcome"

Positive: "marked by, or indicating acceptance, approval, or affirmation . . . affirming the presence of that sought or suspected to be present"

Expectant: "the state of anticipating or looking forward to the coming or occurrence of [change]"

Anticipation, affirmation, acceptance, and expecting the best possible outcome, while asserting the presence of that suspected to be present—what winning attitudes these are! Perhaps songwriter Johnny Mercer had it right back in 1945: "You Have to Ac-cent-tchu-ate the positive, E-lim-i-nate the negative, Latch on to the affirmative, and don't mess with mister in-between" (Time-Life Music, 1989).

These are attributes the counselor wants to transmit and then cultivate within the counselee. To do so, the counselor will gently draw attention to any change, no matter how modest. When change is described, the counselor can emphasize this change through verbal and nonverbal feedback. Any mention of change is highlighted by the counselor's raised tone of voice, excited expressions, and nonverbal positive gestures. Some questions that turn a spotlight on change are: "How did you decide to do that?" or "How do you explain that?" Through such questions the counselee is invited to consider his behavior in regard to personal responsibility and conscious control.

For example, the question "How did you do that?" suggests conscious control over a change that the counselee may not have viewed as significant. One counselee, who said she was feeling depressed, made mention of getting out of her house one morning to go for a walk. "How did you decide to do that?" I asked curiously. "Many other people have responded to depression by staying in their home, often in bed. How did you decide to go out for a walk?" Her responsible decision revealed conscious control that should be encouraged, explored, and elaborated.

The question "How do you explain that?" is asked in a more rhetorical sense. The explanation is not as important as having a spotlight turned on what the counselee is doing that is working. Often the counselee is unaware of the worthwhile things he has been doing. The problem is so oppressive that it is similar to having a hand held up close in front of his eyes. Nothing else can be seen. Drawing attention to statements that describe positive behaviors and thoughts moves the hand back a few feet, revealing more options.

Encouraging feedback highlights the counselee's resourcefulness. This is true of families and couples as well. Recently I met with a family whose preteen son was having difficulty with outbursts of anger. Various approaches had been attempted by the family, all to no avail. Their son sat quietly with his arms crossed during the interview, as his parents spoke about his problem with anger. I asked them about the times when he had gone a whole day without an angry outburst. I could have reduced this time to a shorter period if necessary. His parents made mention of occasions when their son was not angry, so I directed my attention to their son.

"Is that right? Are there times that you are not angry for a whole day?" I asked curiously.

"I guess so," he replied.

"Well, I think that's pretty great. How do you do that?" I asked, seeking to put a spotlight on his resourcefulness. I also said this with rising enthusiasm.

"I just had days where nothing irritated me!" he said with a grin, implying that the answer to his temper was found in others' leaving him alone.

"Really!" I said excitedly, with the sound of sincere wonder in my voice. "That seems like a pretty mature reaction. How do you do that?"

"Well, really, all I mean is that I get my way," he said, assuming that would settle the matter.

"Yet you're not irritated. How do *you* do that?" I repeated myself. "That is something many adults never learn to do."

"Well, I guess I try to be more flexible."

"That's interesting," I said, showing growing interest. "How do you do that, being more flexible I mean?"

"I say to myself that I don't have to get my way this time. I might let someone else go first. For example, I may let my brother go first on the trampoline. Things like that."

"Really! You say that to yourself when you're waiting to get on the trampoline?" I answered enthusiastically. "How do you remind yourself to think this way and not get angry? Isn't that hard to do?"

"It is, I guess," he replied getting into it now. "But I am able to do it."

"That's terrific. And it's also a very mature reaction," I said, seeking to emphasize the significance of such a thought process without being condescending. "Can you think of any other time, either in the past or more recently, that you were able to do this?"

In this way, attention is drawn to change and exceptions. The counselor is assuming that God has been at work in the counselee's life, preparing the way for questions expressing *curiosity*. Encouragement needs to be paced and *fit* with the counselee's own goals and language. If the counselee is not emotionally prepared to recognize the significance of his actions and thoughts, or if the counselor is trying too hard, both will begin responding with the words "Yes, but. . . ."

> When your client or you start to use "Yes, but" or you sense you are trying to talk your client into something, you can suppose you are too far ahead of your client. . . . These situations remind us of a story . . . about a nurse who worked in a physical rehabilitation center. Each day, she would take for a walk patients who were still weak and unsure of the strength of their legs and their ability to walk. The nurse would take them by the arm and begin walking with them down the hospital hallway. She learned that as long as she walked just a little bit behind while supporting the patient's arm, the walk seemed to go well. If she was just a little bit ahead of her patient in the pace of her walking, however, the patient would express uncertainty about walking or say that maybe they were walking too fast. The nurse quickly learned that the walks went better when she was perceived by the patient as just slightly in back, rather than out in front pulling.
>
> *Walter & Peller, 1992, p. 109*

This is also true of counseling in the local church. The counselor can be viewed as attempting to persuade the counselee of meaningful changes that he is not yet willing to hear. Instead of being solution-focused, the counseling session may become *solution-forced*. Attentive listening can be ignored only at the counselee's expense.

LOOKING FOR CLUES

Most counseling interviews begin with questions such as, "So, tell me, what brings you in to see me today?" or even more simply, "So, how can I help?" Any opening that encourages the counselee to *tell his story* is fine. The counselor could even encourage a more outcome-oriented story by opening with the words "What is your goal in coming to see me today?"

While the counselee is talking, the counselor is responding both verbally ("uh huh," "sure," "I see," or other simple sounds of acknowledgment) and nonverbally (nodding or shaking the head, grimacing, smiling). We should not be interrupting the story nor specifically encouraging any greater detail regarding problems.

Not all church counselors are comfortable with note taking, but I do take notes. I will simply inform the counselee I am jotting down bits

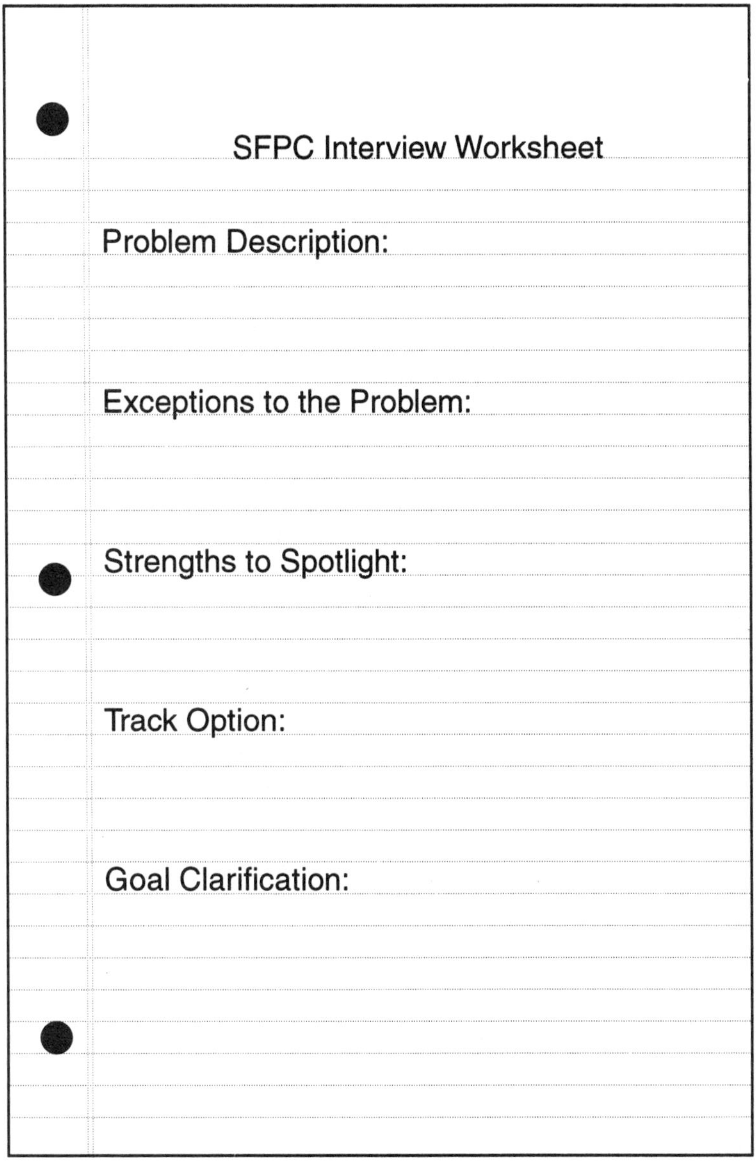

SFPC Interview Worksheet

Problem Description:

Exceptions to the Problem:

Strengths to Spotlight:

Track Option:

Goal Clarification:

Figure 3. Interview Worksheet

of information that I feel are significant in a positive sense and that I will wish to come back to them at a later time. This is exactly what I am doing. I am not detailing problems or developing a social history.

So, what are the "bits of information" that I am jotting down? As you may have suspected, I am looking for any evidence of *exceptions*, i.e., times when the problem was not happening that the counselee has not recognized as meaningful, and *strengths*, i.e., personal, family, or social strengths that the counselee has made use of in the past but is not using now.

Also, I remain alert for any indication of *grace events*, i.e., successful encounters with past problems. These successes should be utilized in preparing the counselee for the next test and for the *writing of the Spirit*, i.e., instances when God has entered the story but the counselee has not recognized as significant. These are used to *inform* the educative aspect of the feedback portion of the interview.

The counselor may wish to use an interview worksheet to help construct solutions. If so, one like that in figure 3 may be used. This is offered only as an example of key elements to look for. My personal notes often look somewhat less tidy. Once I have a basic description of the problem, having jotted down elements of the counselee's story, and having noted initial exceptions and strengths, I use a *track option* (see chapter 11) to begin the process of suggesting alternate perceptions.

AWAITING AN INVITATION

If you want to help the counselee rearrange his furniture, you need first to be invited inside the person's house (Miller, 1995). While jotting down notes, a solution-focused church counselor is specifically looking for moments when the counselee makes any shift from retelling past concerns to speaking in the present or future tense. This shift offers an invitation to the counselor to join in the discussion. Often it will come in the fashion of a request for "expert" help. "So, what would you do, pastor?" "Have you ever heard of a problem like this?" or "What do you suggest, pastor? I guess I'm looking for some advice."

Many times it will come in the form of simple silence, as the counselee looks up to the counselor for help. Or perhaps the counselee will simply shake his head and wonder aloud if there is any hope.

At this time the counselor will suggest to the counselee some of the "clues" that he has noted. It is time then to proceed to a track option. ∎

CHAPTER ELEVEN

Track Options: Highlighting Change As Meaningful

I've learned that to get the right answer you have to ask the right question. *H. Jackson Brown, Jr., 1991, p.146*

Heaven will solve our problems, but not, I think, by showing us subtle reconciliations between all our apparently contradictory notions. The notions will all be knocked from under our feet. We shall see that there never was any problem. *C. S. Lewis, 1961*

Once the counselor is invited into the conversation, the method of selecting a track option can begin. This refers to the second process of the SFPC conceptual schema (see figure 1, p. 107). The intention of each track option is to help the counselor answer questions such as: What will life be like for the counselee without this problem? How would this make a difference? What would be happening when the counselee is on track toward this outcome? What would this track look like? Can this track be described? What would the first step look like on this track? The second? The third? What will need to happen to stay on track? What part of this track is happening already?

God has given each of us a wonderful imagination. *Imagineering* is the ability to imagine a future solution, i.e., what life would look like when the problem is solved. This is a powerful resource, often underutilized in the counseling interview. Even though the solution has yet to occur, it is nevertheless open to investigation. The counselee is encouraged to cocreate with the counselor a gradually clearer *picture of the outcome of counseling*. This supports the initial task of the counseling interview.

Developing a desired outcome begins by selecting a track. I use the idea of the "*track*" in a number of ways. For the counselor, it represents the various avenues along which the counseling interview can proceed. The counselor uses these *track options* as a frame of reference for staying focused in counseling. These are the tracks I will refer to in a moment.

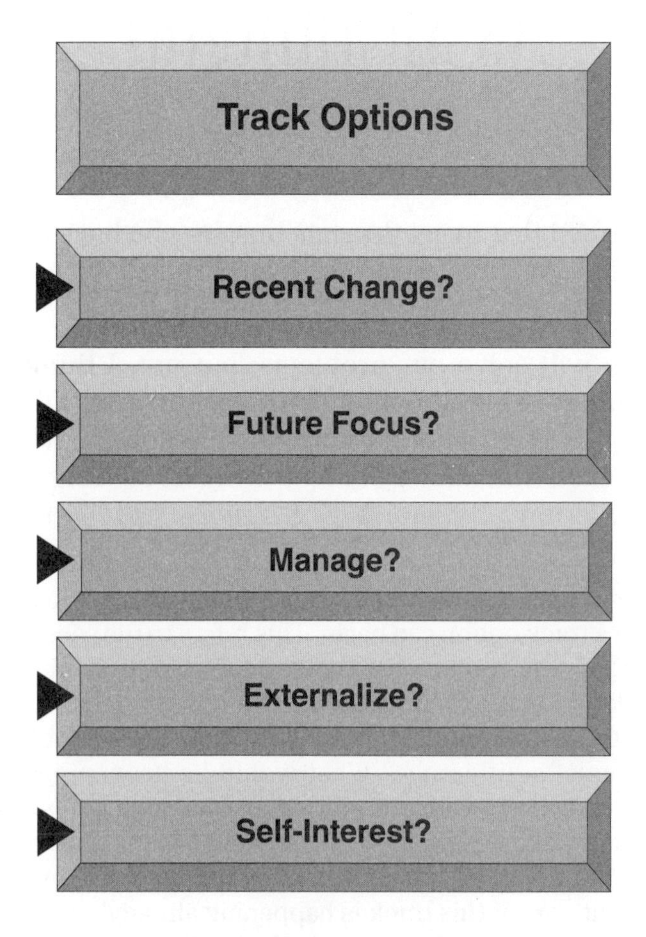

Figure 4. Track Options

For the counselee, the *track represents the actual process of change.* The ultimate destination is the outcome. In this way the counselee can visualize change and improvement, becoming aware of forward progress, and thereby *staying on track.* The track options are represented in figure 4.

RECENT CHANGE

Making a decision to seek counsel may alleviate some of the distress a person is experiencing. There are occasions when doing so lets some of the pressure off. It is as if the individual says to himself, *At least I'm doing something.* The same is often true with marital or family problems. On occasion, the counselee has actually taken steps to correct his difficulties between the time of his first call to the church and arriving for the first counseling appointment, though he may not view these steps as meaningful. If a week or more has passed since the appointment was made, the possibility of his taking such steps increases.

Under the first track option the counselor *assumes* that recent change is a possibility and is curious about what has changed, or is better, since the counselee called. The form of his questioning takes into account the activity of the Spirit, as well as the counselee's strengths and abilities to bring about personal change. This option also *suggests* that a change has already begun. Consider the following example:

Jerry, a thirty-four-year-old single man who is employed with a local firm, has come in to see me. He says he has been depressed for the last few weeks and seems unable to shake himself out of it. He had called last week to schedule an appointment, but the earliest appointment our schedules permitted was for this week. Now upon his arrival he begins to tell his story. While describing the past few days, he implies that he had been busy and had not really had much time to think about how he was feeling.

"Well, tell me, Jerry," I asked, "what have you noticed that's been better these last few days?"

"Well," he answered with a slight smile, "I got out of my apartment more, you know, not just going to work and coming home."

"Hey, that's great!" I replied, cautiously enthusiastic. "How did you get yourself to do that?"

"It's kind of funny you should ask that," he replied. "I was almost home and I decided to pass my exit and go bowling. I hadn't been bowling for years, and I don't know what made me decide to do it. Anyway, I met a few people who attend First Baptist Church, and we got to talking. I ended up having a pretty good time."

When I had said, "Hey, that's great," I was *turning the spotlight* on this exception to his depression and focusing on this change as a change that makes a difference. It is a *meaningful* change, but Jerry had not yet viewed it as significant. *How* questions help to begin the process of clarifying this initial vision of change and allow the counselee the opportunity to enter into this new perception, while recognizing his own resourcefulness. The remainder of the initial interview was spent magnifying and clarifying this and other recent changes—using them in the formulation of a clear counseling goal.

Other questions for Jerry that can draw attention to recent changes, and also encourage clarification, may be:

"How do you account for (this change)?"

"Is it different for you to do these things?"

"What will you have to continue to do to get that (exception to his depression) to happen more often?"

"How did you do that?"

"Are these the sorts of changes you would like to continue to have happen?"

Another way of approaching the topic of recent change would be to ask:

"Many times between calling for an appointment and the first counseling session, people already notice that something seems a little different. What have you noticed about a difference in your (situation, home, marriage, etc.)?"

Note the *suggestion* implicit in this question. I am not asking, "Have you noticed anything?" but rather, "*What* have you noticed?" I am assuming change that may have been overlooked.

All of the questions aim to clarify the vision of life when the problem is not dominating the counselee. (More on "clarifying the vision" after our discussion of track options.)

Some counselors look skeptically, if at all, at any reported recent change. It can be dismissed as superficial—not dealing with the deeper issues. Thus a change may often be overlooked or never noticed at all. Once again, as in Rosenhan's experiment, this is a case of seeing what we are looking for. If we are looking for competence and strengths, we will find them. If we are looking for deficiencies and dysfunctions, we will find those as well.

FUTURE FOCUS

People seldom hit what they do not aim at.

Thoreau

The first track may be all that is necessary to begin formulating and defining a goal. But if there is no meaningful change to report, then the next track is explored. Also, if a counselee presents a *problem-saturated* life description, the counselor may wish to proceed directly to track two. The counselee's focus on problems could be so intense that it is difficult for him to imagine even the slightest improvement.

The second track option constructs a future focus. Through it a creative solution is developed that encourages faith, competence, and a positive outcome. It represents a possible solution that proceeds naturally from the counselee's strengths. In this fashion, faith is projected to the future, creating a hopeful expectation.

Psychodynamic theorist Alfred Adler described an approach similar to this many years ago. He used a tool he simply called "the question." It went as follows: "If I had a magic wand or a magic pill which would eliminate your symptom immediately, what would be different in your life?" Corollary questions were "How would your life be different if you did not have this problem?" and "What would you do if you were well?" (Powers & Griffith, 1987).

William Glasser (1976) also applies a similar approach when he asks, "If right now you had what you want, how do you imagine that your life would be different?" Milton Erickson's concept of "pseudo-orientation in time" also developed this notion of future focus: "These ideas are utilized to create a therapy situation in which the patient could respond effectively psychologically to desired therapeutic goals as *actualities already achieved*" (Erickson, 1954, emphasis added).

> Whereas a problem-focused approach points back to the past, a solution-focused approach is inherently future-oriented. It is grounded in the idea that there will be a time when the effects of the [problem] are no longer dominating. It can be helpful to invite clients explicitly to focus on the future and consider how the discoveries they are making might make a difference.
>
> *Durrant & Kowalski, 1990, p. 98*

Consider the Bible's view of sanctification: an *actuality already achieved*. The Christian is considered as being in fellowship with those who are sanctified. "Now I commit you to God and to the word of his grace, which can build you up and give you an inheritance among all those who are sanctified" (Acts 20:32). The believer is viewed as sanctified by the Holy Spirit (Rom. 15:16) and is considered sanctified *in Christ* (1 Cor. 1:2).

The Christian is perceived as set apart from his old life and sin (1 Cor. 6:11) and his future completion is presented as *accomplished* by God.

> We know that in all things God works for the good of those who love him, who have been called according to his purpose. For those God foreknew he also predestined to be conformed to the likeness of his Son, that he might be the firstborn among many brothers. And those he predestined, he also called; those he called, he also justified; those he justified, he also glorified
>
> *Rom. 8:28–30*

Whatever our theological views on the sovereignty of God are, it is clear that God intends for us to see our future in Him as *already achieved.* This belief informs all biblical preaching. But how can the church counselor use this truth in the counseling interview?

I believe that *anxiety is fear projected to the future.* Fear is spiritual. It was born in the Garden when Adam and Eve first hid from God (Gen. 3:10). This same fear now has all humanity in its grip, for all are hiding. Indeed, it is a spirit of fear (2 Tim. 1:7). Hope is its cure.

Solomon made it clear that "hope deferred makes the heart sick, but a longing fulfilled is a tree of life" (Prov. 13:12).

> Since the future is often connected to the past, people with a stressful past are prone to have a hopeless view of the future. In its turn a negative vision of the future exacerbates current problems by casting a pessimistic shadow over both past and present. Fortunately, the converse is also true; a positive view of the future invites hope, and hope in its turn helps to cope with current hardships, to recognize signs indicating the possibility of change, to view the past as an ordeal rather than a misery, and to provide the inspiration for generating solutions
>
> *Furman & Ahola, 1992, p.91*

Our sanctification is accomplished in Christ. Although sanctification does not free us from hardship, *it is reasonable to assume that sanctification does include life without "distress" from hardship.* What would this life look like? The counselee may have unwittingly *sold his inheritance,* an inheritance that incorporates all that sanctification suggests. The counselor needs to suggest movement toward a future orientation that is more in keeping with the *hope* proclaimed in the Word of God, thereby reclaiming this inheritance.

As described in "William's Story" in chapter 3, the counselor can refer to Romans 8:28 to suggest this future focus. After reading the passage he can propose the following miracle, which is adapted from a question asked by de Shazer (1988): "What if tonight while you are sleeping this passage of Scripture came true for you? During the night a miracle occurred and the problems that brought you here to speak with me are solved. But you were sleeping so you are not aware that this miracle has occurred. Tomorrow morning when you wake up, what will you notice that will tell you that this miracle has happened?"

This opens up an alternate reality of new possibilities. The question requires little explanation and encourages the cocreation of solutions with the counselee. The counselor's task is to assist the counselee to clarify his responses.

"What else would be different when this miracle takes place?"

"Tell me more about that."

"What will you be doing differently when you are (doing the miracle)?"

"What will you be doing differently when you are not (doing the problem)?"

"What will your (family, spouse, child, etc.) notice that is different about you when. . . ?"

The emphasis is on doing. What actions or things will the counselee be doing differently? Feelings are not being ignored or denied, but *to facilitate a future focus it takes less effort to act your way to a feeling, than to feel your way to an action.*

> It is easier to take a new action and your feelings may change. If you wait for a feeling first you may wait a long time. If you try to force a feeling, you may paradoxically produce the opposite of what you want. Anyone who has made an effort to feel relaxed or to feel happier when feeling down knows how counterproductive it is to try to force the feeling.
>
> *Walter & Peller, 1992, p. 78*

The key to getting the most use out of this miracle question is to continue expanding the possibilities, clarifying the vision to develop a well-defined goal. It is not necessarily the miracle question that is significant, but rather the shift in paradigm. This can be encouraged in many ways. Other future-focused questions include but are not limited to the following:

"Let's imagine that our talking together turns out to be helpful. What will you be doing differently then?" (Durrant, 1993).

"Let's step out on faith and say that our time together has been helpful to you. How will you know it has been helpful?"

"Imagine you are on your way home from our counseling session today and our time together has been successful—what would have changed with your situation?"

"How will you know that you will not need to be coming for counseling anymore? What will be different . . . changed?"

"How did you hope I might help you today?"

"What did you hope would be different as a result of your coming here today?"

"Imagine yourself six months or so in the future, after you and I have worked together and successfully resolved the problem that brings you in today. What will be different six months from now that will tell you that your problem is solved?" (Miller, 1995).

Once, when a counselee was in a relaxed mood and had said that he just wanted the problem fixed, I replied in a light-hearted way, "Okay, I'm a pastor, Shazam! It's fixed! What's different now?"

"If coming here was useful, what will you be doing differently?"

"If this were our last time together and you were leaving here with the problem solved, or you were at least on track to solving it, what would you be doing differently?" (Walter & Peller, 1992).

For little children the idea of pretending is helpful. "Let's pretend the problem is solved and you are getting along better with family (or school children or teachers), what would you be doing differently?"

At times this track may come about quite spontaneously. (Indeed, it should always seem spontaneous.) The most unusual future-focus solution I ever offered was to a young couple who came to see me regarding their three children. They had been having a great deal of difficulty with all three, and they were out of ideas as to what to do next. Their frustration was evident in every word they spoke. It was starting to strain their marriage as well.

After listening to their story, I briefly told them of an unusual experience I had had recently. It occurred at my sons' little league baseball game a few months ago. I had the most peculiar notion that I was actually "back in time" watching my now-grown sons playing as children. It was as if I was an elderly man and God had allowed me to pick one day to go back and relive. I had picked this day, and there were my children, little again.

Oh what a thrill it was to see them, not only to watch from a distance, but to interact and to touch their lives once again! As unusual as this may sound, I received it as a gift from the Lord. I realized that, if given the chance to live my life over again, there would be so many things I would do to let them know how special they are to me. Yet here I was. It was today, and the opportunity was still mine. I loved them with renewed enthusiasm, and the day took on even greater meaning.

Then I turned to the parents and asked them to imagine themselves as quite elderly, in the winter of their lives, their children grown and gone. God allows them the opportunity to go back and be with their children again for one day. I asked them what that day would be like for them. They both began to describe, in some detail, what would be *different*. We then clarified that vision as a step toward forming a goal.

Numerous Scriptures can also be used to formulate a future focus in counseling. For example:

"Set your minds on things above, not on earthly things. For you died, and your life is now hidden with Christ in God" (Col. 3:2–3).

"I have been crucified with Christ and I no longer live, but Christ lives in me. The life I live in the body, I live by faith in the Son of God, who loved me and gave himself for me" (Gal. 2:20).

"We were therefore buried with him through baptism into death in order that, just as Christ was raised from the dead through the glory of the Father, we too may live a new life" (Rom. 6:4).

Each of these would be followed by asking something like, "If you died and lived again in Christ, and all the problems that brought you here today are gone, what would you observe that would prove to you that this new life has begun?"

Rejoice in the Lord always. I will say it again: Rejoice! Let your gentleness be evident to all. The Lord is near. Do not be anxious about anything, but in everything, by prayer and petition, with thanksgiving, present your requests to God. And the peace of God, which transcends all understanding, will guard your hearts and your minds in Christ Jesus" (Phil. 4:4–7).

This scripture could be followed by asking, "If a miracle happened this afternoon and you were no longer being controlled by anxieties, but rather had the peace of God, what would you notice that was different? Keep in mind that this miracle transcends our ability to understand it. What is the first thing you would notice that is different?" "What else?"

"No temptation has seized you except what is common to man. And God is faithful; he will not let you be tempted beyond what you can bear. But when you are tempted, he will also provide a way out so that you can stand up under it" (1 Cor. 10:13).

This scripture could be followed by asking, "What would be the first sign to you that God is providing a way out from this problem (or these problems)?"

Sometimes the counselee will answer in a way that seemingly defeats the question, but the counselor must never weaken the miracle. If the counselor is going to continue down this track, he must accept the counselee's inadequate response to the miracle. For example, a counselee may say, "I'd have all the money I'll ever need." Do not back away from the miracle, but use the response as the first step toward constructing a new view of the future. "What would your spouse (children, friends) notice that is different about you if you had all this money?" "What else?"

Or consider this wife who is frustrated with her husband. She comes in to see the pastor without her husband. Her response to the future-focus question showed her to be in a blaming position:

Wife: "I wouldn't have to put up with my husband's complaints anymore!"

Pastor: "What will you be doing when he is not complaining?

Wife: "I guess I'd be more upbeat, more positive."

Pastor: "What else?"

Wife: "I'd be more patient with him." (Now moving toward a willing position.)

Pastor: "When you are more patient with your husband, what are you doing differently?" (beginning to clarify this vision).

I once saw a drawing of an old woman. The instructions told me to look at the picture to see if I could observe anything else in it. Finally, I saw a beautiful young woman with a lovely bonnet. Once my mind made the shift it was easy to continue to see her. So also, once the counselee makes a shift in perception from a problem focus to a future focus, counseling starts to move forward. At this early stage the intention of each question is to suggest a world of possibility where the problem is no longer in charge. The counselee is beginning to regain some control, and the process of defining the goal for counseling can commence.

MANAGING

The second track should lead to the process of describing and clarifying the counseling goal. But sometimes the counselee feels so hopeless or even cynical regarding the possibility of change that he will not respond well to a future-focus question. He is unable to picture life without the problem. Spiritual myopia has set in and all he can visualize are his problems. When this happens, the third track is employed. In the third track option the counselor asks "*managing*" questions.

No matter how creative the counselor has been in looking for clues and strengths or in trying to create a picture of the future, some counselees will declare that nothing is working in their lives and they cannot imagine things being better. The counselor wants to maintain *fit* with the counselee. It is of little use to head off in one direction when the counselee is going another. We want to preserve this agreement with the counselee, mourning, when necessary, with those who mourn (Rom. 12:15). But we also seek to support the intention of the Spirit. Momentarily, the counselor can switch tracks and agree with this hopeless stance. *He can ask questions about how the counselee is keeping things from getting worse.* He can say something like the following:

"It's amazing that you have been able to put up with this. How have you been able to manage?"

"From what you say, it seems the problem is quite serious. How is it that things are not worse?"

"What are you (and your spouse, family, etc.) doing to keep this situation from getting worse?"

"What are you doing to manage when things are so bad?"

"What would tell you things are getting a little bit better?" (Berg & Gallagher, 1991).

Usually, at this point, the counselee will report some aspect of his life that has helped him to get by, even if just barely. These are "exceptions" to the problem. Once he responds with any examples or instances of how he has managed, or why things are not worse, the counselor will want to magnify and draw attention to these exceptions, making them meaningful. Thus, the counselor could say something like:

"How has that been helpful to you?"

"What would it take to make that happen more often?"

"As more of this happens, and things start to get better, what do you imagine yourself doing then?"

"How did you come up with that idea?" or "How did you do that?"

"It seems to me that God is trying to do something to help. What are some of the clues that a little of that is happening right now?"

In the following example, while serving as a chaplain in the U.S. Navy, I used the managing track option with a Navy petty officer who was feeling quite pessimistic about his situation getting any better.

Wade is a twenty-seven-year-old naval petty officer. His wife is also in the Navy and is away on a deployment for the next six months. He is home alone with their two-year-old son. Recently, his older brother was murdered in Detroit. His family wants Wade home for support. Although he has been a fine petty officer, he is now seeking a way out of the service. He is also grieving and struggling with being a single parent. No *recent changes* were reported, and his discouragement is such that he is not able to think of any differences or possible changes a *future-focus* would afford.

Wade: "I just don't see what I'm going to do. I was not able to get a hardship transfer, and I'm just barely keeping it all together."

Chaplain: "I'm amazed you're doing as well as you are, considering the situation."

W: "Yea, I'm amazed too" (shaking his head).

C: "How have you been able to manage?" (shaking my head).

W: "Well, I've been getting out more, I played golf this weekend."

C: "I'm glad you were able to get out for a while. What else have you been doing to prevent things from getting worse?"

W: "I was able to get my son out of a day care where he was very unhappy. I have him in a terrific home for child care now, and he really likes it."

C: "Boy, I bet that's a load off your shoulders. Is there anything else you have done?"

W: I've been going with my neighbor to church, and I've been working on a few continuing education courses" (now warming to the subject).

C: "Hey, that's great! How has that been helping you?"

W: "I guess I feel a little better when I get busy. I usually enjoy getting out with friends."

C: "As you do more of this, and things start to get better, what do you imagine yourself doing then?"

I am always astonished at how quickly a counseling interview can change with this track. Wade did a complete 180-degree turn, and I was able to move the counseling process in a more constructive direction that revealed some important strengths and exceptions. God had been at work as always. From this point on we continued to clarify this vision of the aspects of his life that displayed strengths and personal competence. I eventually taught him how to visualize a track to the future and to move alongside it. More on that later.

EXTERNALIZE

When the managing track option does not yield the desired results, it could be that the problem has become too established for the counselee. He is not able to respond to any of the previous forms of solution-oriented questions, being incapable of creating a future focus where the problem does not dominate. Usually the influence of the problem is subtle, sabotaging any attempt at visualizing life without it. When this happens, the fourth track is used. This track seeks to *externalize* the problem; i.e., the problem is the problem.

The process of externalizing the problem can achieve the following (White & Epston, 1989, pp. 39–40):

1. Decrease unproductive conflict between persons, including those disputes over who is responsible for the problem;
2. Undermine the sense of failure that has developed for many persons in response to the continuing existence of the problem despite their attempts to resolve it;
3. Pave the way for persons to cooperate with each other; to unite in a struggle against the problem and to escape its influence in their lives and relationships;
4. Open up new possibilities for persons to take action to retrieve their lives and relationships from the problem and its influence;
5. Free persons to take a lighter, more effective and less stressed approach to "deadly serious" problems;
6. Present options for dialogue, rather than monologue, about the problem.

When the externalizing track is chosen *it is important not to stay externalized* after the procedure has accomplished its goal. It is then necessary to look for other clues that will lead naturally into the process of clarifying the vision. Otherwise, the counselor may lead the counselee into the subtle error of the recovery movement, with the "solution" viewed as outside itself.

It is also important to maintain *fit*. The way the problem is externalized needs to seem natural to the process of the counseling conversation, using what has already been offered by the counselee. Consider Chuck and Diane:

I had seen Chuck and Diane once a week for four weeks, a lengthy amount of time for my approach to counseling. Even worse, we had made little progress. They had a thirteen-year-old child who had been diagnosed as ADD (having attention-deficit disorder) by another counselor, and they were constantly blaming each other for various problems. They would rarely look at each other in the session, and they often used facial expressions and sounds of exasperation to indicate disagreement with what the other was saying.

In the first interview no recent change was reported, and my attempt to create a future focus was distorted into a position of blame. Each could visualize the *other's* changes but not their own. The session would end with what I believed to be a fairly well-defined goal. Yet somehow, by the time we met the following week the conversation would gravitate in subtle ways back to aspects of blame.

When I realized what was happening, I decided to externalize their blame—moving their focus off one another as the cause of their problems. More important, Chuck and Diane had started to notice the amount of blaming that was taking place, so the *fit* was good.

Counselor: "How long have you two been getting beat up by blame?"

Chuck: "It seems that we are always blaming each other about something. I guess blame has been an issue with us for a long time."

Diane: "That may be true, but you (to Chuck) seem to always start it!"

Chuck: "Here we go again, it's always me! I'm really getting tired of this."

Counselor: (smiling) "Well there *it* is again, popping its head up. It seems like blame can divide you both anytime it wants to. Do you see how it just got between you? How long are you going to let blame get the best of you?"

Diane: (pausing) "You know, that's right; I never looked at it that way before. It seems that blame is always getting between us. It's like it has a life of its own. I hate that."

Counselor: "Tell me Diane, when was the last time blame tried to divide you from your husband, but you didn't let it?"

Diane: "Well, I had a particularly rotten day at work yesterday and I was real tired when I got home. I was hoping Chuck would offer to make dinner, but he didn't. I started to blame him for . . . well . . . for just everything! Then I realized I was being unfair, and I asked him to help me with dinner, which he did" (said smiling at Chuck).

Chuck: "We actually had a pretty good night last night."

Counselor: (enthusiastically raising my hand in praise) "Yes! Now that's a victory over blame! How did you do that?"

The rest of this session focused on times blame tried to divide them from each other and from their son and how they were either defeated or how they gained a victory. Before they left, I asked them to watch for times when they have a victory over blame and to pay attention to how they achieved this victory. I cautioned them that blame had been beating them up for a long time and that they would have to be very alert or it would reassert itself in their lives.

In the next session they felt that they were now on track with what they needed to do. It is interesting that the other matters we had discussed, the future-focused solutions we had cocreated in earlier sessions, were now easier to try. They were very pleased with their victory and had joined forces, so to speak, to fight against whatever may try to divide them.

This approach has the ring of truth to it. Consider Paul's words to the church at Rome:

> For sin, seizing the opportunity afforded by the commandment, deceived me, and through the commandment put me to death. . . . I do not understand what I do. For what I want to do I do not do, but what I hate I do. And if I do what I do not want to do, I agree that the law is good. As it is, *it is no longer I myself who do it, but it is sin living in me*. . . . Now if I do what I do not want to do, it is no longer I who do it, but it is sin living in me that does it.
>
> *Romans 7:11, 15–17, 20*

So our battle is with sin, not with ourselves. *The problem is the problem.* It is externalized. So also, to the Ephesian church Paul writes, "For our struggle is not against flesh and blood, but against the rulers, against the authorities, against the powers of this dark world and against the spiritual forces of evil in the heavenly realms" (Eph. 6:12). The problem is not other people but the deceiving influence of evil acting subtly behind other people. Again, we are freed from seeing the other person, (whether a spouse, child, family member, neighbor, coworker or stranger), as the enemy, or the problem. We can join together with them to fight a common foe. The church is most in agreement with the Spirit when it remembers these truths.

SELF-INTEREST

There will be times when externalizing, or other track options, will not bring about the necessary shift in the counselee's focus. This is often due to the counselee's being in an *attending position*, having come to the counseling interview unwillingly. The counselee could be a child or an adolescent seeing a counselor because of the parents' wishes. Some pastors will also provide counseling for a person who has been ordered into therapy by the courts. There are occasions when an adult will come for counseling simply because family or friends put pressure on him to go. In each case it is not the counselee's intention to be in counseling, therefore he may seem uncommitted and uninvolved. Others, typically parents or teachers, may see this person as needing help but the one *attending* has no goal or agenda to discuss. Nevertheless, the Spirit has brought about the meeting; it is a *divine appointment*, and it is *His* intention we are most concerned with.

With the *self-interest* track option, the counselor seeks to *find out what the counselee's goals are* while assuming that the clues of the Spirit will become evident, given the opportunity. This is not to imply that the counselor should concentrate on selfish, or self-centered needs but rather on the counselee's personal concerns. When a counselee seems uninvolved, it is frequently because his goals are not being addressed, often not even considered.

> We are all most likely to be motivated to work toward goals that we have set and are therefore meaningful for us, and least likely to be motivated to work on goals imposed by someone else. One of the least fruitful activities in which we can engage is to try to convince [someone in an attending position] that he or she has a particular problem. Just because a teacher, or the school executive, or parents have identified what the problem is and what needs to happen does not mean that the [counselee] will agree.
>
> *Durrant, 1993, p. 59*

People who come to counseling may know something is wrong, perhaps even seeing themselves as contributing to the problem in some way. They probably want the situation to improve. The question is, what would be a sign of improvement *to them*? It may be quite different from what the parent, family member, or even the counselor would view as an improvement.

Trying to convince the counselee he has a problem rarely leads to a successful outcome. It usually brings about frustration for both parties. But *something* is a problem for this counselee, and *we need to discover what that is!* The church counselor wants the counselee's cooperation, and this will be possible only when we find out what he wants. "Most adolescent clients tend to cooperate with therapists that pay attention to what *their* goals and expectations are, not just what the parents want" (Selekman, 1993, p. 82).

When counseling those in an attending position, or involuntary counselees, I have tried to keep in mind that any change in the counselee's life will effect change in others around him. I remember listening to the Soviet ambassador to the United States in 1990, shortly before the dissolution of the communist bloc. He said his country was going to do the worst thing it could do to the United States. The Soviets were going to remove our primary adversary—themselves. The statement seemed enigmatic at the time, but it turned out to be prophetic. The dramatic changes in his country dramatically affected our own. As far as foreign policy was concerned, our principal reason for maintaining our national strength and resolve was gone. Also, this dissolution has bred numerous regional and ethnic conflicts that the United States has been drawn into. As a result, we have had to adjust and change as a nation, and we will continue to change.

When small changes take place in a counselee's life as a result of self-interest, it is understandable to think of these changes as self-serving and not as "real" or lasting changes. But just as nations are *interactional*, so of course are people. If an individual begins to behave differently, for whatever reason, his family, friends, or spouse will respond to this change. This sets up a spiral reaction, change in the counselee leading to change in others, leading to change once again in the counselee, etc. Just as problems spiral, action to reaction, solution-oriented behavior can do the same. The first task of the counselor along this track is to *intervene by interrupting this negative reinforcing reaction cycle.*

These are some questions that lead to solutions that inform the self-interest track option:

"Whose idea was it for you to come and see me?"

"Why do you think (the concerned person) wanted you to come and talk with me?"

"Do you agree with what he is (they are) saying?"

"Having someone think you are a problem is a real problem, isn't it?"

"Is there something you want to talk about?" (If there is, continue as with a counselee in a *willing* position.)

(If not): "What do you think would need to happen so you would not need to come back to see me?"

"Is there a time when you weren't doing what (the concerned person is saying) you are doing?"

"What was different then?"

"How did you do this?"

"What do you think others noticed that was different about you then?"

"What do you think (the concerned person) would notice that is different about you when you do this?" (Berg, 1990; Walter & Peller, 1992; Durrant, 1993).

These questions look for exceptions to the problem, strengths that need to be conveyed to the counselee as significant or that seek to redefine the counseling situation within a personal goal. Once the interview begins to focus on a goal that the counselee is more interested in, thereby moving him from an *attending* to a *willing* position, other tracks could be reviewed and followed as well. Additional questions will also be used to "clarify the vision" as with other track options, when a mutual goal begins to become defined.

Here is another counseling situation that will help illustrate this track. The context is once again from my work as a Navy chaplain. This is the case of Petty Officer John Barrows. John was sent to me by his executive officer (XO). The XO's goal was to determine if John was suicidal. He felt Petty Officer Barrows was severely depressed. John had been UA (unauthorized absence) for thirty days. His wife had been unfaithful to him and had now left him, taking their daughter. His career was possibly over, and he was facing legal action. He appeared to be very unhappy (who would not be?) and withdrawn. He did not want to see me and had been ordered against his will to do so. Knowing that this was the case, I went straight to the self-interest track:

Chaplain: "So tell me John, whose idea was it that you come in to see me today?"

John: "The XO told me I ought to come and talk to you."

C: "What makes the XO think you need to talk with a chaplain?"

J: "I guess he wants me to get some help."

C: "Do you agree with him?"

J: "I guess so." (At this point John related some of what had been happening to him, and I listened attentively.)

Since John was already discussing his problem, I did not need to use questions that capitalized on his desire *not* to be in counseling; e.g.,

"What would you have to do in order to convince the XO that you don't need to come back and see me?" I could always ask such a question later if necessary.

C: "This is a lot to be faced with all at once. Have you ever had to deal with real stressful events in the past?"

J: "Not like this."

C: "Yes, this is an awful amount of stress to confront all at once. When you encountered stressful situations in the past, what did you do?"

J: "Well, at work I knew it was something that would end, so I did what was necessary to help resolve it."

C: "How did you do that?" (said with rising interest)

J: "I guess I knew that if I could contain something, I could control it." (his own words!)

C: "Wow, that's good counsel. It sounds like that has worked well for you in the past. What do you think would be different if you started doing a little of that today?"

J: "I guess I never looked at it that way." (said smiling)

C: "What will you be doing differently when you do some of that? What is the first thing you would need to do?"

J: "I would need to work toward a doable solution." (Again, these were his own words! My jaw noticeably dropped.)

The rest of our time that afternoon was spent clarifying this vision of containing and gaining a measure of control over his situation, i.e., cocreating a "doable solution." John eventually left my office with a clearly defined goal. He knew just what he needed to do that day to begin "acting his way out" of this challenging situation.

We met two more times, and after that he was determined to take control of his life once again. The XO and his co-workers noticed a change and responded in a more respectful way, and this reinforced John's resolve. He still had a difficult road ahead, but he considered himself to be back on track, and I agreed.

In a different kind of case, one pertaining to family counseling, a teenager and his parents had come to see me. The parents wanted me to "talk some sense" into their teenage son. You can imagine the potential for success with that operating goal. Instead, I suggested to the teen that it must be really annoying to have his parents constantly on his back. "Having parents think you are a problem is a real problem, isn't it?" Now I was seeing the "problem" from his point of view. This got him talking. He was more than happy to explain to me how unfair his parents were.

I listened supportively and finally asked him what it was that really bugged him about his parents thinking he was a problem. He told me with some frustration that what really bothered him was that his parents did not trust him. They would not let him grow up. After all, he was fifteen years old now! I asked him how this was a problem for him. It was a problem because he was losing privileges and was grounded quite often.

I asked him what will be different when his parents begin to trust him. He began to describe the things he will be allowed to do and privileges he will have. "What will be different about you when this happens?" I asked. He felt that he would be happier in his home, his parents would be happier with him, and so he would feel better too. I suggested that parents are usually pretty difficult to change when they get their minds made up about their kids.

He might have to resort to a kind of "shock treatment" (Tiggeman & Smith, 1989) in order to prove his parents wrong. "It's tough when the kid has to be the one to do all the work, but sometimes he has to because parents get stuck in their ways," I said. (True enough about many parents, I think!) We began to think of ways together whereby he could "shock" his parents this week into realizing they are wrong about him—and that they can trust him (i.e., to prove them wrong). This became his goal, one that grew out of his own concerns, but also had the potential of meeting his parent's goals.

Afterward, I complimented Mom and Dad on their love and concern for their son, and, without losing sight of their son's confidentiality, I suggested that they look for the things this week that he is doing right. In this way they were placed on an *interactional collision course* for potential positive change, which is exactly what happened.

WHEN NONE OF THE TRACKS ARE USEFUL

At this point you may be wondering what to do if none of the above tracks are helpful. My experience is that if you maintain a *tenacious* trust in God's design and preparation, exceptions and strengths will be found and solutions created.

Walter and Peller (1992, pp. 188–98) present some useful approaches, which I have adapted, regarding what to do when the counselee maintains a blaming position, i.e., holding to his belief that someone or something else is the problem. The purpose of each approach is to help the counselee envision a personal goal that can thus be clarified:

1. *Be direct.*

"You know, as much as I would like to help you out, (the other person) is not here, and I know I cannot change (him or her). Is there some other way that I can help you?" If the counselee describes a personal goal at this point, proceed with future-focus track options.

2. *Exploring the future without a change in the other person.*

"What if (the other person) does not change, what will you do?" This question helps the counselee define what he will do that is within his control even if the situation does not change immediately for the better.

3. *Exploring the intent or goal beyond the attempted solution.*

"What are you hoping that will achieve?"

"What will that do for you when (the other person) changes?"

"How will things be different for you when (the other person) changes?" This is once again based on interactional relationship changes. Do some of this now, and the counselee's change will result in reactional change in his environmental context.

When none of the track options are effective, and the counselee continues in either a blaming or attending position, the counselor proceeds past the process of vision clarification to *supportive feedback*, as illustrated in figure 1 on page 107. If the counselee remains stuck in the blaming or attending position after subsequent sessions, the counselor may have to say good-bye, refer the counselee, or state conditions by which further sessions can be continued. Professional therapists know from their therapeutic experience what ministers know from their pastoral experience; that is, just as some people will not be saved, because they *will* not (Luke 22:67), so also, some counselees will not be helped, because they *will* not.

Effectiveness may not increase through use of other counseling approaches when the counselee remains in an attending or blaming position. The church counselor should refer, but often the results are sadly the same. ■

CHAPTER TWELVE

Vision Clarification: A Description of Life Without the Problem

Where there is no vision, the people perish. ▪ *Proverbs 29:18* KJV

I've learned that if you don't feel like being pleasant, courteous and kind, act that way and the feelings will come. ▪ *H. Jackson Brown Jr., 1991, p. 148*

Vision clarification depicts the procedure for describing the counselee's initial vision for a more desired outcome or solution. It consists of assisting him to form a vision of his goal that can be reduced to *small, specific, action-oriented, reasonable, positive, contextual, interpersonal, interactional, and pragmatic* terms. Just as developing a future focus is based on shifting paradigms from a problem to a solution focus, the practice of vision clarification gets to the nuts and bolts of starting along the track toward realizing that goal. Figure 1 on page 107 illustrates this third component of the SFPC flowchart, while figure 5 below develops this process.

We have seen how a picture of life without the problem can be described and various track options utilized to achieve this description. At this point the counselee's initial awareness of a future without the problem needs to be sharpened and clarified. Of course, this process of clarifying the vision will naturally proceed from the track taken. Nevertheless, there are some similarities to each option.

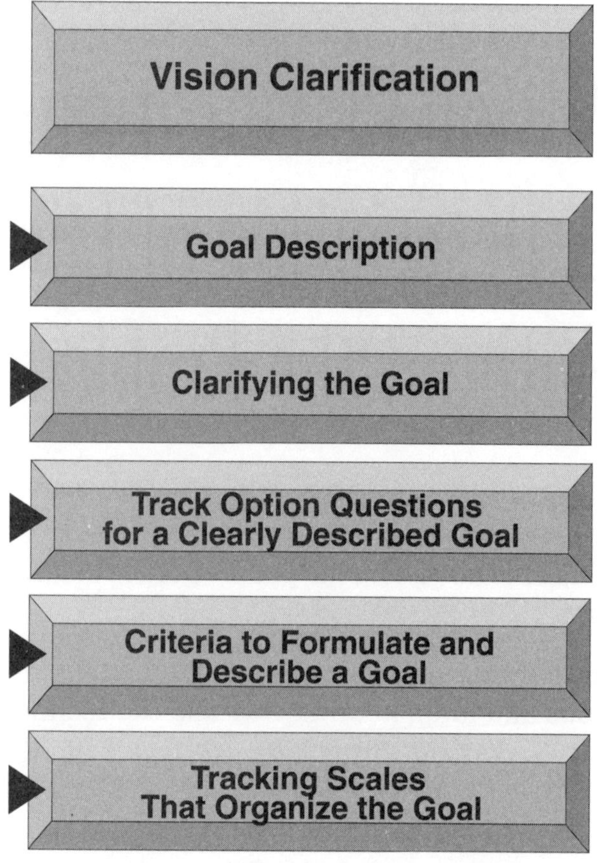

Figure 5. Vision Clarification

GOAL DESCRIPTION

Problem-focused counselors view counseling goals from the perspective of problems or concerns the counselee wants to work on, behaviors he wants to change, or relationship difficulties he faces. No matter how sincerely these goals are addressed, they perpetuate a focus on the problem.

Since SFPC is outcome-focused, it would rather think about what a changed life will be like than to focus on what needs to be changed. What will the future be like without the problem or problems? This is not simply a semantic distinction but rather one that drives the entire counseling session. It suggests an atmosphere of hopefulness from the very onset. It is through the forward movement toward the goal that the counselee's confidence and optimism are encouraged.

This is in keeping with the process of Christian development in general. As Paul proclaimed, "I press on toward the goal to win the prize for which God has called me heavenward in Christ Jesus" (Phil. 3:14). Just as Christian faith is goal-driven rather than problem-driven, so also is the counseling interview.

What helps the counseling interview remain goal-driven is *a clear goal description*. The process of developing this description begins as soon as the counselee starts to imagine a healthy, positive outcome. We want to ask questions that help to *initiate a pattern of future success* rather than focus on past failures. These questions, in turn, help goals to be described in precise terms.

Keep in mind that there is not a distinct line of demarcation from the *track option* to *vision clarification*. One flows naturally out of the other. Forward movement is happening when the outcome is being clarified. As the vision is being articulated, it is being reinforced. I am reminded of this admonition of Paul to the church at Rome: "If you confess with your mouth, 'Jesus is Lord,' and believe in your heart that God raised him from the dead, you will be saved" (Rom 10:9). The counselee also makes a verbal expression—resulting in a clearer description of the future.

Vague goals are hard to evaluate and harder still to accomplish. For example, a goal such as becoming *happier* is hard to evaluate, since happiness is such a personal concept.

Consider Bob and Alice. They are a young couple who came to me seeking advice. They had been married for one year. Bob did not know if he should take a job he had been offered in the area because his wife wanted to move back to Cleveland where her family lived. It turned out that this issue was now seriously influencing their marriage. When I asked how it was affecting them, Alice began to weep.

A few tissues later she said to me, "I just don't want to be so sad all the time." I asked them a future-focused question and received only nervous shrugs. So I rephrased the question by asking what would be different if they did not have a problem right now. They answered simultaneously; Bob said, "We'd be happy," just as Alice said, "We'd be in Cleveland!" What would be different in Cleveland I wondered. All Alice could say was that she would be happier there. Bob said he would be happy if Alice was. Some counselors may view this as indicative of an emotionally dependent statement. I thought it revealed a potential for encouraging more solution-driven *interactive* behavior.

I asked Alice, "*When you are happy, what will you be doing differently*?" "Well," she answered, "I won't be sitting around the house so much." Alice did not have a car and therefore stayed in the house, since she did not know anyone who could provide transportation for her. "So you would have a car in Cleveland?" I wondered. "Well, we have a car, I just can't drive it," she replied. At this point I discovered that Alice could not drive her husband's car because it had a stick shift. After a few more questions I learned from her what would be different if she was happy. She would be driving, getting a job, and making new friends. From this point it was easier to clarify her goal, which would need to include learning to drive and getting a job.

It turns out that Alice was unhappy because she was isolated. Through her own shift to a future focus she determined that her goal was not to move to Cleveland, but rather to become more independent and have a fuller life. What started as a vague goal was starting to become more defined, even as it was being described. With the beginning of an achievable goal, her countenance changed dramatically. This change also *rubbed off* (interaction) on her husband, who at about this time was wondering how he was going to teach his wife to drive the stick shift!

Specific goals that provide a sense of "how we will know when we get there" (de Shazer, 1988), are an important step to promoting the possibility of a solution. They often help the counselee realize that some of what is necessary is in part *already* happening.

CLARIFYING THE GOAL

So what else needed to happen in order to more fully describe and clarify this couple's goal? Although the issue of moving to Cleveland was still an option, it was no longer urgent. *Moving back home was a means to an end. We went directly to the end, or solution, which turned out to be to promote independence. We then sharpened that picture.*

There are various methods for achieving this. Other solution-oriented counselors have asked questions such as, "If I had a video camera and could see you living without this problem, what would I see?" Or, "If I were a fly on the wall in your home, what would I see when you are living without this problem?" (O'Hanlon & Weiner-Davis, 1989). (Hopefully not a flyswatter!)

What these methods have in common is that they seek to clarify the initial vision. So I explored with Alice, "When you are learning to drive and looking for a job, what are you doing differently?" With some personal emphasis Alice replied, "I know one thing, I won't be sitting around the house all day being unhappy!" It is interesting that she already had a different picture of herself than she had only moments before. This shift is important and needs to be developed.

This is now the process of *cocreating* a solution with the counselee. I do this based on the assumption that God's Spirit is already actively encouraging forward movement in her thinking, carefully crafting and supporting her personal growth. I specifically avoid discussion of deficiencies.

"I wonder, are there times when you do get out *already*?" I asked. Alice went on to explain that she does go for walks and had recently had a nice visit with her neighbor. I wondered what other times, either in the past or in recent weeks, she may have had these kinds of enjoyable experiences. Alice told me of other times she had gone out, as well as times she stayed around the house but felt pretty good.

In order to help her see this change as *significant*, which it was, I asked, "What's different about the times when you do this?" Alice's answer was spoken with growing insight: "I guess these are the times I make up my mind not to just sit around and feel sorry for myself." Now I had never implied that Alice was feeling sorry for herself. Nevertheless, this seemed to be a meaningful realization for her.

To further clarify this growing vision of what her life is like when she is happy, I asked, "How are you thinking differently when you do that?"

"I'm not blaming Bob, or anything like that," she answered. "I'm taking responsibility for myself and I'm not *beating myself up* so much."

"I'm curious, how does Bob see you as acting different when you're thinking this way?" I asked. Alice and Bob went on to *describe* in some detail how Alice acts different when she is *happy*, that is, when she is behaving and thinking in the ways already described. I continued to ask questions such as, What else? How do you do that? What is different when you do that?

Finally, I asked Alice to imagine a track to her future. "On this track is a scale of 1 to 10. Ten is at the end of the track and represents your life when you no longer feel isolated and are being more independent." As I was saying this, I was pointing down an imaginary track. "Number 1 represents how bad things were when you and your husband called for an appointment. Where are you on that track right now?"

Alice said she was at about a 3. Speaking with enthusiasm, I responded by asking her how she had gone from a 1 to a 3 in the short time we had been talking. Alice's response is significant. She said she *felt* more confident about what she had to do *next*. She felt more empowered and had a picture in her mind of what she needed to do to get back on track. Small change often leads to greater change. I heard somewhere that *wisdom does not consist of knowing what to do in an ultimate sense, but in knowing what to do next.*

In order to create a connection between her personal changes and the goal for coming for counseling, I asked her, "As you continue to do these things, will you think you are on the beginning of a track to getting what you hoped for when you came here today?" In this way the goal becomes the continuation of these changes.

After taking a break and offering *supportive feedback*, Alice stated that her goal was to move from a 3 to a 4. We clarified specifically what this would entail. After we prayed together I encouraged them both to observe when Alice was "doing a 4 or above." When she was, they were to make a mental note of what was different—not only for Alice but also for Bob and other relationships. I made this suggestion to reinforce their focus on strengths and competency. They agreed, leaving my office with a clear vision of the goal as well as a plan for how to move toward it. A second and last session continued this process.

Follow-up revealed that Alice was still on track months later. She was actively making progress toward her goal and continued to feel confident about the process. In addition, Bob was much more satisfied with his life now that Alice was doing so well. He had become even more supportive of her *change*, which reinforced this change for Alice. This is a healthy, interactional circle.

TRACK-OPTION QUESTIONS FOR A CLEARLY DESCRIBED GOAL

All of the track options have the purpose of coaxing an initial shift in perception. The aim is to create a preliminary description of life without the problem. When this description, or vision, is clarified, the counselee begins his journey, *walking out* from under the weight of his problem.

Repentance has been described as making a 180-degree turn. Imagine a room in which one wall represents God and the opposite wall represents sin. The goal for Christian growth is not defined by our struggle to stay *away* from the *sin* wall. Rather, the goal is better understood as walking toward the *God* wall. When the Christian does the latter, he quite naturally walks away from the sin wall.

So also, when I make a long trip, I first form a clear picture of the journey in my mind, perhaps consulting a map. Once I am on the journey the road signs declare how many miles I must travel to get to the next city. I noticed this forward-looking focus one night during a long, exhausting trip home. I had grown quite tired while on my way to Virginia Beach from Richmond, Virginia. The road signs did not tell me how far I had gone *from* Richmond; rather, they told me how much closer I was to my home in Virginia Beach. I was able to take heart as I drew closer to my home and a good night's sleep.

I could also gage my progress by the mile markers—similar to a scale of 1 to 10. The picture of home grew clearer as I drew closer. What I needed to do was stay on the right road, or *track*. If somehow I got off the highway, the chief task would be to get back on—not to figure out *why* I got off the road. In order not to repeat the same mistake, I may also study my map to determine *how* I got off. But even more important is to remember *how* to get back on!

In this way, the counselee begins the process of walking out from under the weight of his problem by creating a clear picture of the destination or goal. Various questions are asked to *connect the track option with vision clarification*. Remember the "bits of information" that were jotted down earlier in the interview? We were looking for any evidence of *exceptions*—times when the problem was not happening that the counselee had not recognized as meaningful, *or strengths*—personal, family, or social strengths that the counselee had used in the past but was not using now.

Other information jotted down included the *writing of the Spirit*—times when God is perceived as entering into the story, but the counselee has not appreciated the significance of that—and *grace events*—past problems, successfully encountered that should be used in preparing the counselee for the next "test." These inform and explain the exceptions and strengths. That is, the Christian recognizes that, as Paul said, "when I am weak, then I am strong" (2 Cor. 12:10). Our strengths and exceptions are due to a loving Savior's continual intervention. Apart from Him we can do nothing (John 15:5).

In connecting the track option with vision clarification, these clues are once again considered. Questions are also used to continue bridging the initial change in focus to a fuller description that can be used as the goal of counseling. The purpose of the questions below is to encourage a *progression* of the process of clarification. *This progression creates an observing approach to life, rather than a reacting one.* Most stress-related emotional issues are reaction oriented. *Deliberate action and observation* tasks will play a major part in the *supportive feedback* portion of the interview.

Any track option can ask these questions to encourage progression. Any question can be used in another track. I offer this breakdown only to show progression and to simplify the process, not to lock the counselor into a regimented set of questions. If the counselor listens carefully, he can use the counselee's own choice of words to frame his selection of questions. The questions presented here are neutral in character. That is, they would need to be *fleshed out* by the counselee's own words.

Some recent change-track questions that encourage a progression of the initial change in focus are:

"How do you account for (this strength)?"

"Is it different for you to do (these exceptions)?"

"What will you have to continue to do to get (that exception) to happen more often?"

"How did you do that?"

"Are these the kinds of changes you would like to continue to have happen?"

Some future-focused track questions that support continued change are:

"What else will be different (in the future solution)?"

"Tell me more about that."

"What will you be doing differently?"

"What will your (family, friends, etc.) notice that is different about you when this happens?"

"What will you observe about them as they react to your doing a bit (of the solution)?"

"What will you be feeling when you are doing a bit (of the solution)?"

"How will your (family, friends, etc.) know you are feeling (this way)?"

"What will (they) see you doing that is different?"

"Are there times when small pieces of (the desired outcome) happen just a little bit now?"

"What is different about the times when that occurs?"

"What will have to happen for you to do it that way more often?"

"What does your (family, friends, etc.) notice that is different about you at those times?"

"Who else notices?"

"How could you tell (this person) noticed?"

"How did you decide to do this?"

"How is that different from the way you have handled (this situation) recently (or in the past)?"

"So what would it take for you to make (that) happen just a little bit?"

"What else?"

"What will be the first sign that you are on track to getting a little better?"

"As you continue to do these things, would you see yourself as being on track to getting what you wanted when you came to see me?"

The purpose of the managing track is to promote a shift of focus from problem to solution in individuals who report that nothing is working for them and that they cannot "imagine" any change. Once the shift is made, questions from the *future-focus* track are used.

Some other managing track questions that support continued change are:

"I'm amazed you're doing as well as you are, considering the situation. How have you been able to manage?"

"What are you doing to manage when things are so bad?"

"How have you managed to do that?"

"How has that been helpful to you?"

"What would be a sign that things are getting a little better?"

"What would it take to make that happen?"

The purpose of the *externalizing* track, like the managing track, is to promote this same shift of focus from problem to solution. It can be used at any point, but I use it when people report that nothing seems to be working for them—they cannot "imagine" any change, nor are they responsive to the managing track. Again, once the shift is made, questions from the *future-focused* track are used.

Some other externalizing track questions that support continued change are:

"How long have you been getting beaten up by (this problem)?"

"How long are you going to let (this problem) get the best of you?"

"When was the last time (this problem) tried to get the best of you, but you didn't let it?"

"How did you do that?"

The purpose of the *self-interest* track, like the managing and externalizing tracks, is to promote this same shift from problem to solution-focus. In this case it is utilized primarily with those who are in an *attendee* position. This individual will typically be unresponsive regarding the previous tracks. As before, questions from the *future-focused* track are used to clarify the vision once the counselee has shifted to a *willing* position.

Some other self-interest track questions that support continued change are:

"Whose idea was it for you to come and see me?"

"Having someone think you are a problem is a real problem, isn't it?"

"What do you think would need to happen so you would not need to come back to see me?"

"What do you think (the concerned person) would notice different about you when you do this?"

"How will you know you have done enough?"

"Who will be the first to notice the changes when you make them?"

"What would (that person) do differently when you do this?"

"What difference would this make in your relationship with (this concerned person)?"

"What is the first step you are willing to make to get started?"

"How will you do this?"

What are the means I use to develop these questions? I use five specific *criteria* to help formulate and describe a goal. These are adapted from Walter and Peller's guidelines for defining a goal (1992, p. 60). I also use *tracking scales* to help visualize forward motion, clarifying a picture of continued change. Both criteria and tracking scales connect the initial shift in focus to a fuller goal description. Keep in mind, the counselor should use the counselee's own choice of words to shape all questions.

CRITERIA TO FORMULATE AND DESCRIBE A GOAL

1. Questions that create a hopeful depiction
2. Questions that seek specificity

3. Questions that describe personal action
4. Questions that empower
5. Questions that create a track

1. Questions That Create a Hopeful Depiction

These questions encourage a response from the counselee that begins the process of what he will be doing *instead*, rather than what he will not be doing. I am reminded of the saying, "I don't smoke, drink, or chew, or hang around with those who do." Okay. So now we know what this Christian does not do, but what *does* he do? Christian faith is not about what we must not or cannot do, but about what we *can* do in Christ. It is optimistic, expectant, heartening, and hopeful.

It is futile to try to describe what a counselee will not be doing. Indeed, it is not possible to get an image or picture in our minds of what we will not be doing or thinking. It is like being asked *not* to think of a purple elephant with pink polka dots. What are you thinking of right now? In this way, when a counselee expresses his desire not to be arguing with his teenage son anymore, it is useless tying to depict not arguing. The only picture that comes to mind is the father and son in an argument.

I once heard it said that there is not enough darkness in the world to put out the light of one candle. Why? Darkness is the absence of light, it has no substance. So also, a goal expressed in the negative has no substance. It cannot be imagined. What it can do is reinforce a focus on the problem. Therefore, when the counselee expresses his goal as what he will *not* be doing, the church counselor wants to encourage a hopeful depiction—what he *will* be doing.

For example, if the counselee states he does not want to argue with his son anymore, the question to ask would be, "So what will you be doing *instead*?" We are more concerned with the presence of something rather than the absence of something.

2. Questions That Seek Specificity

In a recent mystery movie a detective was asking questions of a witness to a crime. His questions helped clarify the witness's memory of the event. By the time the inquiry ended, the detective had a pretty clear picture of what had happened. He then asked the witness to give a description of the criminal to a police department artist. Again the investigation began, culminating in a picture of the criminal that the witness did not at first feel capable of giving. It was the skillful use of questions by the detective and the artist that clarified the picture *for* the witness.

The skillfulness and artistry of the counselor is of primary importance here. *As the detective seeks to clarify the memory of the event for the witness, so the counselor seeks to clarify exceptions, strengths, and creative solutions.* What will the counselee be doing? What will he be saying? What will he be thinking? What will others be doing and saying? This cocreation of the solution is crafted, one piece at a time. In the end a clear picture has materialized. It has proceeded *from* the counselee, but it was the artistry of the counselor that brought it out. From this picture proceeds the goal description and initial encouragement to take the first small step toward that description.

When seeking *specificity*, the counselor should ask questions that include such words as: *specifically*, *exactly*, and *precisely*. For example, "Can you tell me more *specifically* how you and your husband will be communicating when you are on track?" "How, *exactly*, will you be doing this?" "Tell me *precisely* how your husband will be doing this?"

3. Questions That Describe Personal Action

"Ready! Places! Action!" Thus the shooting of the movie begins. It's not a still picture but a moving picture. It describes action. So also, the picture that we want the counselee to form in his mind is not a still picture but a moving picture. Someone once said that *love is a verb.* The solution is also a verb, or rather, is described in a verb tense expressing continuing action.

Questions that help the counselee to form this moving picture begin with the word "how." "*How will* you be doing this?" This will elicit from the counselee responses that depict his own action or the action of others. For example, an often unresponsive husband could be asked, "*How will* you be showing your wife that you love her in a way that she will feel loved?" He could respond by saying, "I would be *hugging* her and *looking* into her eyes more." "We would be *going* out on dates more often, and I'd be *treating* her with respect." All of these responses depict actions. In reply to a "how" question this husband is describing what he will be *doing* and is therefore creating a clearer picture of the goal.

4. Questions That Empower

When a counselee is in a blaming position, he views himself as unable to make a difference in the situation. He does not view himself as part of the solution. It is the other person that needs to be different.

The other person is defined as the problem. The counselee views himself as waiting helplessly for the other person to change. The other person must change before the relationship can change. The counselee needs to be empowered to envision a goal that he can begin to move toward, even if the other person does not change.

> Clients often think that in order for "B" to happen, "A" has to happen first. Acting in accord with this assumption, they persist in trying to make "A" happen so that they can have "B." However, if "A" is outside of their control, they can end up very frustrated.... When clients state a goal that is out of their control as a means to something they want, we help them reverse the assumption about the means to the end. Where clients think that "A" leads to "B," or "A" has to happen first, we often suggest the opposite assumption, that "B" can lead to "A." Very often, "B" involves some action or change of thinking on their part which is within their control.
>
> *Walter & Peller, 1992, p. 57*

For example, a man was frustrated with the instruction to love his wife. He viewed love as primarily emotional in nature, and he had not felt love for his wife for some time. From his point of view he was being asked to feel an emotion that he no longer experienced. This was beyond his control. He wanted to save his marriage, but how could he do so when he no longer "loved" his wife?

In this case, *A*, feeling love, was viewed as necessary before, *B*, a restored relationship, could occur. The suggestion was to act on *B* first, in the hope that it would lead back to *A*. So the questions would emphasize what the counselee will be doing when *B*, a restored relationship, is an actuality. Thus the question to this husband could be, "What will you be doing differently when you do feel love for your wife?" This creates possibilities that are within his control, thereby empowering him to work on the goal. It is not possible for him to feel his way into loving behavior, but loving behavior may rekindle his loving feelings.

5. Questions That Create a Track

Many of those who have come to me for counseling characterize their goals with a far-away description. The goal is something they want to do—eventually. I want to describe the goal as something they can get on track with upon leaving the initial interview. So if a couple come in wanting to help their marriage, I want them to be on track toward a clearly described goal when they leave. I may ask, "If you were *on track* to strengthening your marriage, what would you be doing differently?"

This encourages them to focus on things they can do right away. They may also discover strengths they are already using.

Whenever the goal is too far in the future to be of any practical use, questions are used to create a track: "What will be the first sign that you are *on track* to getting a little better?" "As you continue to do these things, would you see yourself as being *on track* to getting what you wanted when you came to see me?" Remember, movement along the track characterizes forward progress in counseling.

TRACKING SCALES THAT ORGANIZE THE GOAL

Tracking scales are used to help visualize forward motion, assess progress, and clarify the picture of change. In this sense they *organize* the vision for the counselee. He is able to visualize both where he is at the present time and where he is going. Tracking scales are used to measure numerous characteristics. They assess hopefulness, willingness to work toward solutions, recent change, self-esteem, and commitment to relationships, to name just a few.

The counselee's answers to the scale are not related to external standards of mental health, as most psychological tests are. They relate entirely to the counselee's *internal* perceptions. Further, they *assume* change.

> The scale builds on the assumption of change in the desired direction. Since a scale is a progression, the number "7" assumes the number "10" as well as "5," "3," or "1." It also assumes movement (or change) in one direction or another, rather than stagnation. By virtue of this, an expectation of change is built into the process of asking scaling questions.
>
> *Kowalski & Kral, 1989, p. 61*

The value of a tracking scale is in how it is used by the counselor. It needs to fit the counselee's own goal formulation, using his own words. Also, the numbers are not absolutes. They are analogous to the *counselee's* view of his own situation. The counselor can encourage the counselee by offering support *no matter where* he places himself on the scale.

The basic form of a tracking scale is shown in the following question: "On a scale from 1 to 10, where 10 means how you want things to be, and 1 means the worst that things have been, where would you say you are right now?"

I use a similar form as a *tracking question* to assist in visualizing the track to a created solution. That is, it helps to envision the desired outcome, as well as indicating where the counselee views himself in relation to that outcome. The way the tracking question is presented must *fit* the counseling conversation. For example, in chapter 3 I wanted to establish William's willingness to work toward a cocreated solution. You may want to reread this case vignette.

I asked him, "Imagine a scale of 1 to 10, with 10 meaning you have confidence that all the things you have described can be accomplished, and 1 meaning you have no confidence at all, probably because of alcoholism, PTSD, and possible loss of job and family. On that scale, where would you put yourself today?"

William answered by saying he *was* a minus 1 when he had entered my office that day. I did not question the accurateness of his answer, whether it was right or wrong—it was a springboard into more change talk. His use of the word "was" implied some change already. This is what I proceeded to ask him about. He related that he was hopeful that his situation would improve. By rephrasing the outcome expectation through a second scaling question, William settled on a 5. I could have debated the wisdom of this number; perhaps it was too high. But the five meant something quite specific *to* William, and that was what was significant. He now perceived himself as able to do something positive. He viewed himself as empowered to make a difference.

As we neared the completion of our time together I asked him, "When you're doing a little of (this projected outcome), do you think that you will be on track toward a solution to your problem?" This more precisely created a picture of William's position on the track and his willingness to continue toward the described goal.

Besides being used as a tracking question, tracking scales can be used at any point in the counseling interview to *fit* the counselee's personal situation. Once the individual conceptualizes his track, solution-focused questions can be used to clarify the vision.

Tracking scales can be used to assess a level of commitment to a relationship:

"On a scale from 1 to 10, where 10 is 'I will do anything to save our marriage,' and 1 is, 'I have given up on this marriage,' where would you put yourself at the moment?"

They can assess whether the counselee is in a willing position and is committed to work toward solutions:

"On the same scale, with 10 meaning you will do anything to solve this problem, and 1 meaning you will sit and wait for something to happen, where would you put yourself today?"

They can be used to encourage and envision forward progress:

"On the same scale, with 10 meaning how you hope your life will be when you solve the problem that brought you here, and 1 meaning how bad things were when you called for an appointment, where would you say things are today?"

"That's a good deal of improvement. What did you do to be (at that number)?"

"What would have to happen to move to the next higher number?"

They can make reported recent change more meaningful:

"On the same scale, with 10 meaning how you will feel when your problems are solved, and 1 meaning how you were feeling when we first spoke together, where would you say you are today?"

"How did that happen?"

They can be used to clarify specific goals:

"On the same scale, with 1 meaning I don't feel like I can get any of my homework done, and 10 meaning, I feel like I've got it all together with my homework, where would you say you are today?"

"What would have to happen to move to the next higher number?"

They can be used to assess self-esteem:

"If 100 means the kind of person you always wanted to be, how close would you say you are to 100 today? What is the closest you have ever come to 100?"

"On a scale of 1 to 10, with 10 meaning I'm very happy with my place on the 100 scale, and 1 meaning I really dislike where I am on the 100 scale, where would you be today?"

"What would have to happen for you to move up on the 100 scale?"

They can be used to encourage communication:

"On the same scale, how much do you think your spouse wants this marriage to succeed?"

"What would your spouse have to notice different about you for him/her to say that you are moving up to the next highest number? What would he/she do differently then?"

They can be used to capitalize on strengths and exceptions:

"Since you are at a 6 on the scale of wanting the marriage to succeed, what is the highest you've ever been? When was that? What were you doing then? How did that make things different?"

They can be used to create a future-focus:

"Since you are a 4 on the scale of wanting your marriage to succeed, let's imagine that you come back to see me in a couple of weeks, and you tell me that you have moved to a 6 on the scale. What will be happening differently then? What will you have done to move yourselves from a 4 to a 6?"

Once again, vision clarification consists of assisting the counselee to form a vision of his goal that can be reduced to *small, specific, action-oriented, reasonable, positive, contextual, interpersonal, interactional, and pragmatic* terms. It gets to the nuts and bolts of starting along the track toward realizing the goal by crafting a goal description, clarifying that goal, and utilizing questions that proceed naturally from the initial track option that was effective. The counselor makes use of specific criteria for clarifying the goal and tracking scales for organizing the goal. ■

CHAPTER THIRTEEN

Supportive Feedback: Promoting and Supporting Change

> The tongue has the power of life and death.... *Proverbs 18:21*

> Therefore encourage one another and build each other up, just as in fact you are doing. *1 Thess. 5:11*

> Even if you are on the right track, you'll get run over if you just sit there. *Will Rogers*

The fourth component of the SFPC flowchart (figure 1, page 107) represents the final process of the counseling interview. It comes after the counselor takes a break so that he and the counselee can assess what has happened thus far. Each can then give feedback to the other and determine what, if anything, should be done after the interview. Figure 6 below magnifies the segment of the flowchart relating to this process.

As we have seen, ongoing encouraging feedback characterizes the attitude of the counselor throughout the counseling interview. Yet *supportive feedback* represents that particular aspect of the counseling interview that comes after the counselor and counselee pause to collect their thoughts. A short break is taken to encourage reflection regarding what has been said in the interview. The break gives both counselor and counselee some time to think through what would be helpful.

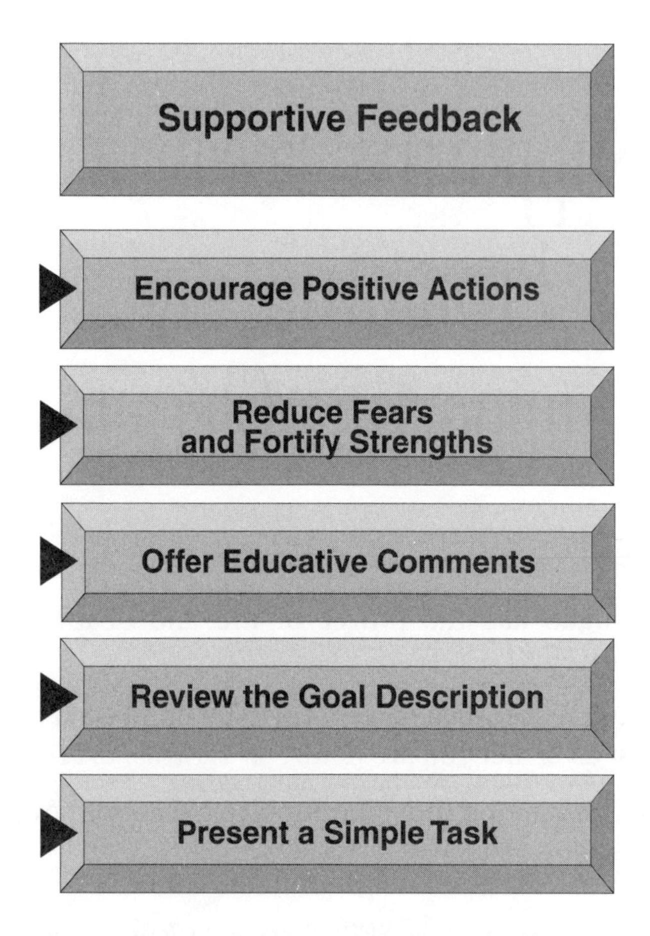

Figure 6. Supportive Feedback

The professional therapist needs to put a specific time limitation on the counseling interview. It is not financially realistic to do otherwise. Church counselors are not under this financial constraint, but most are under time constraints. I have had some "marathon" counseling appointments, as most pastors have. God has often moved in a significant way right at the last minute. Yet many times, once a reasonable length of time has passed, both counselor and counselee become fatigued and unfocused. Although I try not to put a specific time limit on the counseling interview, experience has shown me that twenty to forty minutes of conversation is usually sufficient to highlight change and visualize an initial goal.

After an initial goal is formulated, the counselor announces a break. Remember to prepare the counselee for this pause when the interview begins. Let him know that you will step out of the room for a few minutes in order to consider what has been discussed up to this point, and that you will return with some suggestions and feedback. I also propose that the counselee consider what has transpired to this point and let me know when I return if anything comes to mind that might be helpful. I often tell the counselee, "It will probably be the kind of thing you would remember or think of on the way home in your car."

Remember that ongoing encouraging feedback helps to create a counseling environment that is affirming, hopeful, and optimistic. Throughout the interview the counselor has been looking for evidence of the work of the Spirit. Strengths, exceptions, *grace events*, and the *writing of the Spirit* all require use of the creative imagination. The counselor encourages an atmosphere of H.O.P.E.—i.e., a *Hopeful*, *Optimistic*, *Positive*, and *Expectant* counseling climate. A counselee who thought he was doing everything wrong will often respond to such a climate, making statements such as, "Well, I guess I'm not as bad as I thought I was," or, "I'm doing something right after all," or, "I didn't think anything was working in our marriage, but I guess we're doing a few things right," or, "I just thought I was crazy."

Instead of feeling overwhelmed, as a counselee often does at the conclusion of a problem-focused counseling session, he or she is more positive and expectant of change. Keep in mind what God said through the prophet Jeremiah: "'For I know the plans I have for you,' declares the LORD, 'plans to prosper you and not to harm you, plans to give you hope and a future'" (Jer. 29:11). Hope refers to a sense of expectancy: the future will be better than the past or even the present. Faith is expectant!

This type of emphasis is maintained during the break. The benefit of taking a break is found in giving the counselor time to step back from the process of sustaining the counseling dialogue and to think more concretely regarding feedback that will be supportive. When the counseling interview is in process, the counselor is more concerned with *fit*, clues, and directing the conversation toward goal construction. During the break the counselor is no longer constrained by these tasks. He can now deliberate in regard to creating a solution from the goal description.

The break also permits the counselor to brainstorm regarding his notes, forming them into usable educative comments or tasks. It allows him to rest from the concentration the interview demands. Sometimes

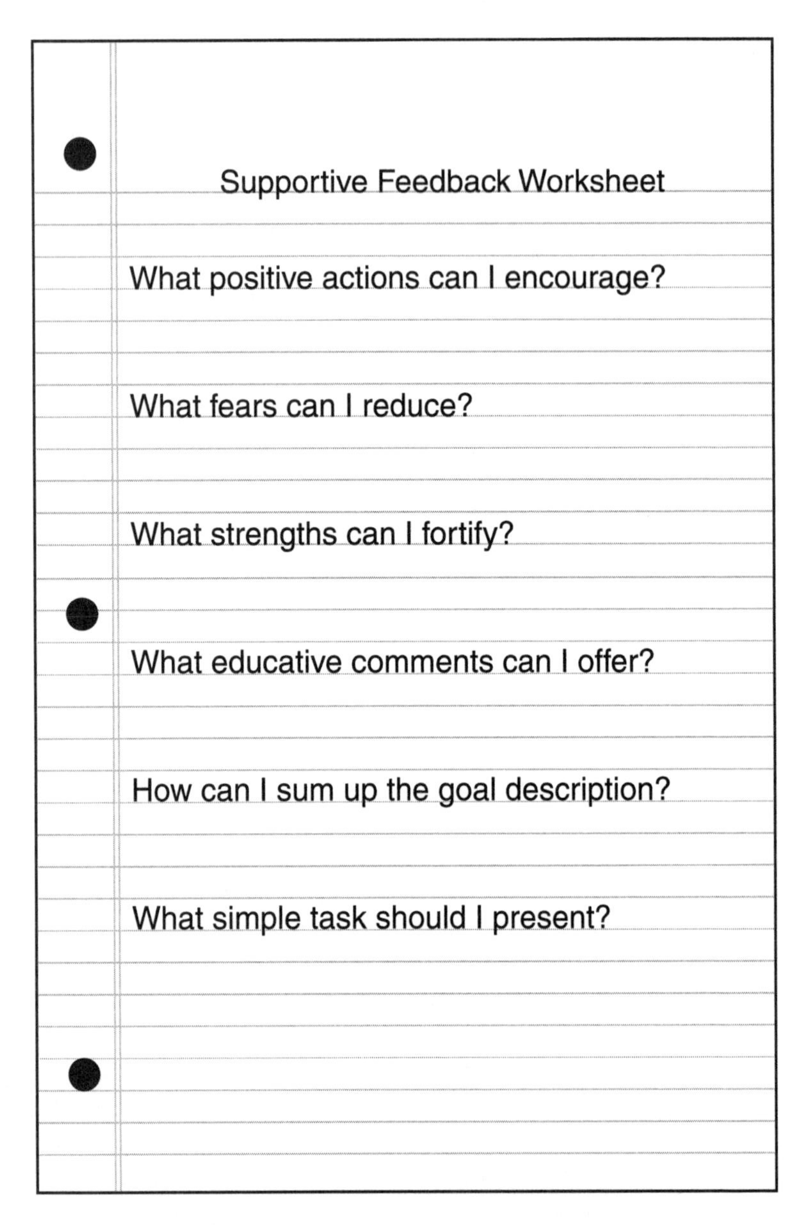

Figure 7. Supportive Feedback Worksheet

the counselor can get too caught up in the interview; he needs to step back to get perspective.

There are five areas to be considered during the break in order to prepare supportive feedback. Figure 7 offers a worksheet for organizing this response. The five areas are these:

1. Encouraging positive actions
2. Reducing fears and fortifying strengths
3. Offering educative comments
4. Reviewing the goal description
5. Presenting a simple task

ENCOURAGING POSITIVE ACTIONS

During the break the counselor will review his interview worksheet notes, looking for specific details. The first selected are those that will encourage any positive actions observed in the counseling interview. This will draw attention to those actions and reinforce them. Immediately upon returning from the break, the counselor should be ready to praise the counselee regarding even the slightest positive action. This is not to be confused with flattery. *Praise and compliments are offered for actions, thoughts, and behaviors that reveal the counselee's commitment to the purpose of counseling.* Even the smallest amount of commitment needs to be encouraged.

For example, a family came to me with concerns about their teenage daughter. They were no longer confident in their parenting or in their daughter's ability to change. Nevertheless, during the interview several examples were given of the parents' determination to help their daughter, even when they seemed to be at the end of their patience. There were also some tender moments when their love and concern were expressed. The daughter was quite attentive and interested by session's end. She did not say much, but she was willing to work toward a modest goal. These positive actions were not initially viewed as meaningful by the family. In my supportive feedback I complimented the parents on their expressions of love and support, and their daughter on her attentiveness. I began my feedback by saying to the parents:

"I am very impressed by the love and support you have shown in this interview. It is clear to me that you deeply love your daughter. Your daughter has made it equally clear that she does not always feel loved. This often happens between parents and their children. It will be necessary for you to learn how to communicate to her in a way that helps her to be sure of the love that you both obviously feel for her. But you are here, and you have demonstrated how much you want to support your daughter and to strengthen your family. I want to congratulate you on your commitment."

To their daughter I said, "I am very much impressed by your willingness to come to this counseling session with your parents. That demonstrates maturity. You could have blown this whole thing off by either refusing to come or refusing to participate. You did neither. You are here, and you have chosen to get involved in coming up with a solution for both you and your parents. I want to congratulate you on your willingness."

In this way, I encouraged any positive actions I had observed in the counseling interview—no matter how small. This kind of encouragement influences a counselee to think in this way as well, not only about himself but also about others. It sets the stage for further development of solution-oriented thinking and perspective. It reinforces what is positive and thus stimulates the counselee to think about change as something he is already doing.

Praising the counselee for any observed positive actions also accomplishes two other functions: (1) it helps to *normalize* the problem and (2) it *reinforces counselee responsibility*. Regarding the first, there are times a counselee feels as if he is alone with his problem. He may wonder if there is something wrong with him or if he is the only one who is experiencing a problem like this. In offering praise and encouragement the counselor is suggesting that no temptation has taken hold of him except what is common to us all (1 Cor. 10:13).

When I said, "This often happens with parents and their children," I was not trivializing the parents' struggle. Rather, I was *normalizing* it. I was suggesting to them that there was nothing wrong with them as parents, or with their daughter for that matter. In this way the problem was *reframed* and competency was reinforced. Remember—the problem is the problem. Praising the counselees for the positive actions already taken allows them to take the pressure off of themselves and to see the problem as something that many people go through. It discourages the desire to place blame. *Normalizing* can also be used to *reframe* potentially discouraging moments during the interview.

Regarding the second, the counselor is giving the counselee encouragement in doing what has worked. This *reinforces responsibility*. From the very beginning, the counselor is giving credit to the counselee for any perceived changes. It is not the "expert" counselor who takes the credit and who must be returned to when future problems arise. This would be a mistake, as it can foster dependency, which is certainly not the goal of counseling. Rather, the changes come because the counselee is making them, and he is acting within God's grace. Honest praise and compliments for observed positive action allows the counselee to take credit for such actions. It also discourages a refusal to take responsibility for changing.

REDUCING FEARS AND FORTIFYING STRENGTHS

There are two fears that can paralyze a counselee: the *fear of change* and the *fear of rejection.* The fear of change and the difficulty of change or the fear of the consequences of change can be minimized by the counselor as he proceeds at the counselee's pace. Change is inevitable, but it is often frightening. It represents the unknown, and each small step forward needs to be met with encouragement and praise. Just as each small step of an infant is met with words of support and encouragement by his parents, so also each effort by the counselee, no matter how small, needs to be recognized and praised. My words of praise are usually directed toward the counselee's perseverance and determination.

Yet from the perspective of church counseling, the fear of rejection may be the more debilitating for the counselee. "Clients often feel exposed and fearful of the judgment an 'expert' may be going to make" (Walter & Peller, 1992, p. 116). This was written within the context of professional psychotherapy. It may be of even greater concern within the context of a visit to the pastor or other church counselor.

The enemy has planted many foolish notions about judgment and criticism proceeding from the church and so giving Christian counselors a reputation that many tend to live *down* to. What will the counselor's response be to admitted sin? Certainly we do not want to trivialize sin. But we do want to *normalize the experience of sin;* i.e., we are all in the same boat. There are none among us who can legitimately "cast the first stone." We have all been forgiven much and must therefore be ready to treat others as we have been treated by God.

When the counselor begins his feedback with compliments, along with words of encouragement and praise, the enemy's strategy is defeated. Instead of receiving criticism from the minister for weaknesses and sin, as many may fear, the counselee receives hope and praise for even the smallest reported strength and exception to the problem.

For example, a man in his mid fifties came to see me regarding his marriage. His job required him to be away from home, often for months at a time. Now, after twenty-two years of marriage, he feels little love for his wife. He says she has "let herself go," and he is no longer attracted to her. Even though he believes she still loves him, he is considering asking for a divorce. This past year when he was away from his wife, he committed adultery. He has been wrestling with a guilty conscience because of his actions.

Does he need to go outside of the church to discuss his unfaithfulness? Can the church counselor, who often is the pastor, keep this kind of information confidential? Keep in mind, the man is showing no true signs of repentance and certainly little remorse at this point. A Catholic priest has clear guidelines regarding the confidentiality of the confessional, even if the confession is insincere. Protestant ministers should be, but sometimes are not, as clear about a counselee's confidentiality.

In this case, I recognized that the counselee was still in a *blaming* position, not yet willing to see the responsibility for change as being within himself. As strongly as I felt about the wrongness of his actions, our conversation could quickly come to an impasse if I concentrated primarily on his adultery. My intent was to help him visualize a healthy outcome and to take the next step that would allow him to begin to reach it—not to pass judgment on his adultery. I could offer plenty of advice, and some should certainly be offered whether asked for or not. After all, I do not cease to be a pastor when approached personally for counsel. But even advice can be offered from within the context of his strengths. After the break I began by saying:

"You knew I would be up front with you about the sin of adultery when you came to see me, and I have been. Yet I am impressed by your openness and honesty this evening. I can see that you are now struggling with a difficult transition, whether to go forward with God and rebuild your marriage, or to continue living with lies and possibly losing your marriage.

"I also think it took a great deal of courage to come and talk to me in the first place. It shows that this is an issue that you are very serious about. You clearly have the determination to follow through once you make a decision. The questions before you this evening are, Which direction is your life going to go? Are you going to go forward with God or continue in your direction away from Him? If it is forward with God, what will your wife and children notice that is different about you? These are questions you will need to answer."

Before he left I asked him to observe what happens in his marriage, as well as his relationship with his children and with the Lord, that he wanted to have continue. He took all of this to heart and came back to see me nearly a month later. He had been doing some serious wrestling with this decision. He started by saying:

"I've been struggling with what we talked about last month. I want you to know that I was very apprehensive about coming to see you. When you stopped to take that break at the end of our talk I was really sweating. I was thinking that you might return and, you know, ask me to leave the church, or something like that.

"When you told me how much you appreciated my honesty and courage in coming to see you, well, I was glad I came. You told me to think about all the things I have, and what I would lose if I chose against God. I realized that I was at a turning point in my life, and I needed God's help."

I was thankful for how God's Spirit had moved in his life. Perhaps there is some similarity here to Jesus' response to the woman caught in adultery (John 8:10–11). She was fearful of His judgment. This fear was quickly reduced. Her strength was also fortified in an almost too obvious fashion. When Jesus said to her, "Neither do I condemn you; go and sin no more," He was *assuming this woman's competency.* Jesus would not tell her to do something that she would be incapable of doing. He showed no interest in discovering if she had a dysfunctional childhood or if she was living in a codependent relationship. No. "Sin no more" is built on the presupposition that she had the strength to fulfill such an injunction.

OFFERING EDUCATIVE COMMENTS

> I've learned that if you pursue happiness, it will elude you. But if you focus on your family, the needs of others, your work, meeting new people, and doing the very best you can, happiness will find you.
>
> *H. Jackson Brown, Jr., 1991, p. 30*

This statement and many others like it offer *alternative reasoning*, i.e., a new way of viewing a situation. Educative comments help to inform the counselee, enabling him to put his problem into a larger context. The counselor wants to illustrate the solution to encourage alternative reasoning. For example, what have professional studies and research revealed about this problem? How can a new perception of this problem be encouraged through the use of God's Word?

As we have seen, praise and encouragement help to empower the counselee and to move him beyond his fears. Educative comments are intended to illustrate and inform change. This is an area in which pastors and teachers are proficient. We learn to connect certain illustrations with certain passages of Scripture. Or we offer a new perspective to a situation that is informed by personal faith. I have often quoted Proverbs 3:5–6 to encourage *eternal vision.* "Trust in the LORD with all your heart and lean not on your own understanding; in all your ways acknowledge him, and he will make your paths straight."

Here we are told *not* to lean on our own understanding. Why? I believe it is because we do not see the whole picture regarding our own lives. But God does! So we trust and acknowledge Him in all we do. This encourages alternative reasoning for the reader of God's Word. Indeed much of Scripture is in the business of doing this very thing. It is calling us to a new perception of reality, of our lives, families, challenges, and problems.

This new perception should inform our educative comments. For the most part, such comments are just that—comments. They are short statements, reserved for the closing minutes of the counseling interview. Unfortunately, for some church counselors, the entire session is made up of one illustration after another, one scripture after another, one anecdote after another. It seems that throughout the session the counselor is trying to persuade the counselee to alter his way of thinking.

Pastors do tend to get wordy. My congregation knows I do, but they love me anyway—thank God. We preach to persuade, and we are used to this freedom in our pulpit ministry. This is one reason why many pastors make poor counselors. They have not developed the self-control needed for *attentive listening.* Proverbs 3:5–6 is also true for the counselor. He may not see the counselee's "whole picture," and, with the best of intentions, he is sometimes doing little more than giving a spiritual pep talk. The counselee is being treated to a "mini-sermon," and he does not even need to give an offering.

The church counselor should not be in the business of convincing. This is an often tiring way to counsel; believe me, I have been there. We may take more and more responsibility for the success of the interview, and the counselee takes less and less. If we are not careful, we can spend much effort trying to get the counselee to see an answer that seems obvious to us. "I'll just try one more illustration, or one more scripture," we say to ourselves. Then, if the counselee does not respond, we may give up and conclude, "He's just not ready to get serious with God."

Save these "messages" for the educative portion of the interview and keep them brief. Clarifying the vision and developing a well-described goal should be the primary considerations. Although I sometimes use educative comments during the counseling interview, I have learned that no matter how meaningful they seem to me, they often disrupt the session more than help it. Instead, jot down reminders to bring up such comments during the *supportive feedback* portion of the session. Some may no longer seem as urgent, and new ones may emerge. It is at the end that they will have the greatest impact.

These comments are chosen to help clarify and secure any noticeable gains in counseling. For example, in counseling an individual who was now preparing to take his first small steps out from a painful loss of a relationship, I used an illustration referred to earlier in this book. I made the following comments:

"The Chinese word for crisis is very interesting. It is the word *weichi. Wei* means danger, and there is great danger in a crisis. But *chi* means opportunity. What you are going through represents one of the most drastic and abrupt changes that an individual can encounter. This kind of change often results in a personal crisis. Keep in mind that in the midst of change there is both danger *and* opportunity. It is our responsibility to find and use the opportunity side of this loss.

"Remember what Paul said in 2 Corinthians 1:2–4: 'Grace and peace to you from God our Father and the Lord Jesus Christ. Praise be to the God and Father of our Lord Jesus Christ, the Father of compassion and the God of all comfort, who comforts us in all our troubles, so that we can comfort those in any trouble with the comfort we ourselves have received from God.' You are going to be formed by this crisis. It is up to you to determine how you are going to be formed. This week ask yourself what the first thing will be that your family will notice about you that is different when you are being comforted by God."

During another counseling interview, the counselee had applied our Lord's instruction "Love your enemy" to loving someone in his family. I had jotted this down in my notes. He was having great difficulty loving someone whom he considered an "enemy." He simply could not feel love for this person. During the feedback I made the following comments:

"I want you to consider that there is more than one word in Greek to translate the English word *love*. The word for love of family, or child, is *storgē*. This is a natural love, most strongly demonstrated by the feeling of love a mother has for her child. It remains undiminished even when it is not reciprocated. This is also the kind of love we have for our families.

"Yet the word used by Jesus for love is *agápē*. This is quite different. It signifies a choice, a decision to love. It is more clearly demonstrated by actions than by feelings. In this way you can act in a loving way toward someone you have no *feelings* of love for. You can actually love someone you dislike. Thus when Jesus said, 'Love your enemies, bless them that curse you, do good to them that hate you, and pray for them which despitefully use you, and persecute you' (Matt 5:44 KJV), the first step in love was already indicated—to pray for them. This is an action, not a feeling. When you are praying for (this individual) during the week observe what is different about how you are thinking about him (or her)."

To another counselee, who had mentioned during the interview that he was quite upset over things that were happening at his job, I said, "Sometimes it helps to view the situation as if it is a coin. There are two sides to a coin. In your case, the first side would represent the job. That is, something you may not have a lot of control over. The second side represents your reaction to the first side. Let's work on this second side, since here is where the changes are completely within your control. Then we can look back at the first side and see what changes you can make within the system. At that point you may observe that some changes have already occurred within the system in response to the changes you have made within yourself."

To parents who had mentioned concern over how "different" their son was from them, I said:

"I have on occasion used a children's test called a Messinger-Briggs Type Indicator. What I have discovered is that children from the same parents can often be quite different from their parents in personality type. Hopefully, their character has developed through their parent's good and consistent example, but their identities are all their own.

"I remember one child who tested as being very creative, flexible, and spontaneous. He loved the excitement of inventing and starting a new project but wasn't as concerned with finishing it. This drove his parents to distraction, since they were very organized, structured, and deliberate. They loved nothing better than checking off a finished project, sometimes checking off projects finished earlier just for the pleasure of checking them off!

"As long as they viewed themselves as the standard for normalcy, their son would always be considered abnormal. Actually, he was simply different from them. He would have a creative and exciting life, but he needed to receive encouragement and unconditional love from his parents. From what I have observed, your son is quite different from you. But God is leading him along his own path. He will also have a full and abundant life, and you can come into agreement with God's plan by making sure he feels loved and by continuing to be a consistent example of God's grace. You may want to consider this week what will be a sign to him that this is happening. What will your son notice that is different?"

As you might imagine, their son no longer wished to be adversarial with parents who showed such consistent love and support. In turn, his parent's love and support were reinforced when they observed their son in less adversarial terms. This sets up the positive, interactional circle within the family system.

REVIEWING THE GOAL DESCRIPTION

I have mentioned the five types of questions that are used in formulating a clear goal description. They are (1) questions that create a hopeful depiction, (2) questions that seek specificity, (3) questions that describe personal action, (4) questions that empower, and (5) questions that create a track. When the goal description is reviewed, it is the last time within the counseling interview that the picture, or video, of what the solution will look like is viewed. It is a mental review, or role play, of what the counselee will be doing instead of what he had been doing. What will he be doing specifically? How will he be doing it? What is it that he will be doing differently? How will he know that he is on track?

Thus during the break the counselor is recreating the main steps the counselee has already taken during the interview to describe the goal. The criteria that were used are considered and drafted into a clear but brief goal description that can then be rehearsed with the counselee. For example, for the parents who were going to try to help their son to feel more loved, I may help them summarize and rehearse their goal in this way:

"During the break I tried to summarize what we had discussed regarding your goal of helping your son feel more loved. You said that you usually showed your love by providing for his physical needs and you both felt that this should be enough, but it hasn't been. Since it isn't working, you have decided to try doing something different. You mentioned that you wouldn't be assuming that he feels loved by you, but *instead* you would be *specifically* going out of your way to tell him. *You will* be finding time to get out alone with him individually, to make loving eye contact as often as possible, to touch, hug, and hold him often each day.

"Dad, you said you would be grabbing hold of him from behind and gently swinging him around a little. Also, you mentioned gentle wrestling and doing other "guy" stuff. You both said that you would *not wait for him to do anything first* but that you would choose to continue to act in this way and observe how the Holy Spirit leads in healing the relationship. On a scale of 1 to 10, you both felt you were at around a 3 in doing these things right now and you were going to try to move that up the track to a 4 or a 5."

In this way, the goal is being clearly described—and agreed upon—one more time before the counselee leaves. In this case, these parents were getting a chance to clarify the vision one more time. Remember, this is a vision that has come out of their own lives and experience. The goal is a natural result of asking solution-focused questions, narrowing down and clarifying that focus, and doing a small part of the solution to observe what happens. This, then, leads us to the final segment of the supportive feedback.

PRESENTING A SIMPLE TASK

Along with encouraging positive actions, reducing fears and fortifying strengths, offering educative comments and reviewing the goal description, supportive feedback will offer a task that will encourage the counselee to do a part of what he envisioned during the interview. Again, it is easier to act your way into a feeling than to feel your way into an action. And again, as Will Rogers said, "Even if you are on the right track, you'll get run over if you just sit there."

The task will focus on actions, specifically acting out a part of the solution that has been clarified. Traditional homework is often problem-focused. If the counselee fails to do the assigned homework, it is viewed as resistance or a lack of commitment. Also, when the homework is left undone, it creates an atmosphere of deficiency and frustration.

Tasks, unlike traditional homework, are based on something the counselee has clearly envisioned or is already partly doing. It is also somewhat ambiguous: it leaves room for the counselee to "flesh it out" through his own actions. The purpose of the task is to encourage success, along with a "ripple effect" (Bateson, 1980, p. 50). The ripple effect refers to the *interactions* that continue the positive process of change after the counseling sessions end.

Tasks will be tailored to the counselee's level of motivation. The level of motivation is best gauged by the position the counselee is in at the end of the interview. If he is in a *willing* position, he is likely to be ready to take action to help bring about the change he wants. The task will be built on what the counselee is doing that is working and what he can clearly visualize. Tasks are varied and creative. Normally the counselor will suggest a task that proceeds naturally from the perceived solution. At other times he will choose from various solution-focused tasks that are available and will be discussed in a moment.

If the counselee is still partially in the *blaming* position, he may have been skillful at describing and observing what is necessary for someone else to do. But he has not been as successful at clarifying what *he* will need to be doing differently in order to bring about change. Again, supportive feedback will encourage any positive actions, it will seek to reduce any fears and fortify any strengths, and it may offer educative comments. But the description of the goal is not reviewed, because it has not been achieved in the counseling interview.

This does not imply that the interview has been a failure. But the necessary paradigm shift has not yet been achieved and the task needs to be given with this in mind. Few of the solution-focused tasks will be applicable. In this case the more ambiguous the better. The counselee could be asked to consider or observe something about his situation that may lead toward solution, usually something positive. For example, the *Formula First Session Task* may be used here successfully. The counselor could say, “Between now and the next time we meet, I would like you to observe, so that you can describe it to me next time, what happens in your family that you want to continue to have happen.” Then in the next session the counselor can begin, from these observations, to look for a track into a more clearly described personal goal.

If the counselee remains in an *attending* position, supportive feedback will probably be limited to complimenting the counselee for what he is doing that produced even the slightest amount of positive movement. It may be praise for simply showing up. Keep in mind that this person does not feel he has a problem that needs to be taken up in counseling. The purpose here is to remain accessible, keeping the door open. If and when he returns, the intention of counseling will be to discover a personal complaint or problem that can be addressed and used to create a solution-oriented goal. A task would not be appropriate in this case.

When tasks are suggested, they will be solution-focused, and they will flow naturally from the goal that has been envisioned—*using the words and concepts of the counselee*. The tasks are usually observational in nature. That is, they are *not* assignments that need to be structured, completed, and brought back to the next counseling session. Rather, they are based on the following activities:

- Doing a small piece of the envisioned goal
- Looking for what works
- Intentionally doing more of what works
- Observing what takes place when you do so—i.e., interaction

This is easily remembered as *deliberate action and observation* (del/ob). For example, to the parents who, on a scale of 1 to 10, both felt they were around a 3 in reaching their described goal and were going to try to move to a 4 or a 5, I said:

"What I would like you to do this week is to do whatever it will take to move up to a 4 or a 5 on this scale. It will probably be a part of what you have already described. I want you to take notice of what is helping. You don't need to write anything down, just make a mental note. Whatever you do to move along the track and you find that it is helping, I would like you to intentionally do some more of it.

"Again, I would like you to take note of what happens that is different when you do so. That is, what is different within yourselves emotionally, and what do you notice that is different with your spouse and your son? When we next get together, I want you to let me know what you noticed. Okay? Great!"

A number of things can happen with a del/ob task. First, the parents have been empowered. They know just what they want to do, and it is something that came out of their own lives and experience. They can own this goal, and therefore they can own the task as well. Second, the task is in their own words and grows out of their own described solution. Third, a natural by-product of observing is to not *react*. Most negative interactional circles occur through reacting before thinking. Observing often forces an increase in clear thinking about a situation. Fourth, positive interactions are encouraged. Fifth, if the parents notice positive change, they will have a means of subjectively measuring their progress. They can see forward motion on their own scale. This also encourages greater effort toward the goal.

This is the primary type of task used in SFPC when counselees are in a willing position. There are many other solution-focused tasks that could be used, some of them have already been mentioned. The following five can be used with each of the track options. You will notice the common element for all of them is observation.

1. Find Out How Changes Happened

With the *recent-changes track*, changes often seem spontaneous to the counselee. These changes may be quite recent or they may represent exceptions that have occurred over the past months. In either case, you may hear statements like, "It just happened," or, "I don't know, I just felt better on that day." The counselee does not see it as within his control, nor can he explain how it occurred; therefore he cannot deliberately repeat it. Thus the task becomes finding out how these changes take place.

Here the counselee becomes a detective, searching for clues as to why things went better on a given day. For example, a woman who is usually depressed but reported in counseling that for half a day last week she was not depressed would be asked to explore what was different that day. This could be tied in with a modified pretend task. On one day this week she could pretend she felt the way she did on that day when she was not depressed. She could observe what happens when she does this. What was she doing? What was she thinking? Did she notice anything different? Did anyone else notice anything different? Take note and do more of it. See what happens.

2. Pretend

C. S. Lewis wrote, "All mortals tend to turn into the thing they are pretending to be" (1942). Although said with malice by Wormwood in *The Screwtape Letters*, it is true all the same.

When I was in college, a roommate talked me into wearing a costume as a gag for Halloween. When I did, I was astonished at my *change in personality.* I was wearing a full rubber mask of an old man, old baggy overalls, and large boots. I walked all over the campus, crooked and stooped over, dragging one foot, and only mumbling. All evening my fellow students were trying to figure out who I was. No one would have ever guessed who it was, because this was so unlike me. In a sense, I became that crooked old man for a couple of hours. I slowly followed Dawn, my soon-to-be bride, all over the campus that night. Every time she turned around, there I was creeping up behind her, with the emphasis on creep! I was quite comfortable in my alternate identity.

Pretend tasks could be used with a *future-focus track.* With pretend tasks the counselee gives himself and others permission to act as if the solution, and its clarified vision, have already been accomplished. This will allow the counselee the freedom to jump right in with both feet and begin behaving differently right away. When applicable, I will encourage others among family and friends to look for differences in the counselee. This adds an element of fun to the task, and it gives the counselee *permission* by these "others" to change.

3. Do Something Different

If what you are doing is not working, stop doing it and do something different. Sometimes we all get into unhealthy habits. A mother says such and such in a certain tone of voice, with certain nonverbal motions. A daughter responds in *that* tone of voice with *those* nonverbal motions. Then the counselor says, "And don't you just hate it when she does that!" Of course, this is a negative, reinforcing, *interactional* pattern. As with the dancing mother described in chapter 6, changing the action affects the interaction. When all else fails, just do something different. Sometimes the change may be quite silly. This task could be offered to those who have started to develop their creative solution through the *managing track.*

A young married couple once came to see me. After three years of marriage they had begun to argue often. As we discussed this, it turned out they had sometimes *managed* by changing the conversation or by planning a romantic evening. We discussed how this was different for them. Then, on the principle of doing more of what was already working, I suggested they do additional things that are different whenever they began to fight. I told them about another couple I had read about who had a similar problem with arguing. Their counselor encouraged them to pause whenever a fight was starting and go together to their bathroom. There they could continue their argument—the husband sitting in the bathtub dressed only in his birthday suit, and the wife sitting on the toilet seat in her "all together." As we were laughing about the image this brought to mind, they decided to try it as well!

In reporting back at the next session, they started nervously giggling when I asked about what was better. It turns out, they simply could not treat each other in a mean or cruel way while in those positions. The pattern had been so drastically altered that they had no serious confrontations that week. Feeling more empowered by how *they* were able to do this, they explored other options by which the same outcome could be achieved. The key was that the solution for them came out of their own experience.

I have always believed this is why Peter said, "Husbands, in the same way be considerate as you live with your wives, and treat them with respect as the weaker partner and as heirs with you of the gracious gift of life, so that nothing will hinder your prayers" (1 Peter 3:7). Couples cannot both pray and remain angry. Prayer drastically interrupts the negative interactional cycle.

4. Strategies for Defeating the Enemy

A number of things can be done once a problem has been successfully *externalized.* The counselee can be asked to take note of everything he does when he is winning against the problem. Some individuals have made up 3x5 cards with lists of what they do when they are successfully defeating their problems. They can then look at these lists as a reminder on difficult days.

This can be done with couples and families as well. Perhaps you recall the couple I had been seeing who were "getting beaten up by blame." Eventually they kept track of all the times they successfully joined together to defeat blame. This encouraged a more deliberate and positive focus for observations to be made.

5. Detecting Hidden Change

In families who are in a willing position and whose children have been approached along the *self-interest track*, the children can be asked to do a few of their own described solutions at times during the week—without drawing attention to what they are doing. Their behaviors would proceed from the goal description privately arrived at in counseling when the parents were not present. Also, they are not to tell their parents what the hidden changes are going to be.

The parents are told to keep their eyes open and, like detectives, try to notice all the occurrences of change that will take place that week. They are directed not to tell the children that they have been found out and are asked to report back the following week. These roles could also be reversed.

I have had occasions in which parents came back with long lists of positive things their child had done during the week, only to have the child tell me in private that he had not participated after all. When the parents became aware of this, they realized that there are numerous positive behaviors to be discovered, even without the child's full participation—once they make an effort to notice them. Once again, we all tend to find or see what we are looking for. ■

CHAPTER FOURTEEN

Second and Later Sessions: Consolidating Change

Nothing succeeds like success. ▪ *Alexander Dumas the Elder*

Solution-focused pastoral counseling (SFPC) treats each session similarly. In the second session, and later sessions if necessary, the counselor evaluates the counselee's progress. The counselor's primary responsibility will be to *highlight*, *support*, and *consolidate* gains, turning a spotlight on any reported change. The process of clarification begins once again, after which the counselor will seek to assist the counselee in consolidating his progress. Unless there is a need for the counselee to retell his story, this part of the session will move as swiftly as possible into change talk.

When the counselee returns for a second session, he will report that either things are (1) better, (2) the same, (3) worse, or (4) there has been a setback. If counseling has been for a family or for a couple, they may not agree as to whether there was any progress. *Each position should be respected and used as the initial entrance back into solution-oriented conversation.*

It is helpful to keep the following thoughts in mind:

1. Assume that there have been helpful positive changes.
2. Highlight these changes by asking for details.

3. Support change as meaningful.
4. Consolidate these changes.
5. Ask what other changes have been helpful.

Instead of asking how things have been or how the counselee is feeling, remember these presuppositions; the counselor should encourage solution-focused conversation. It is important not to slip into deficiency language in the second session. A way to avoid this is to start the conversation by asking questions such as these:

"What is better since the last time we got together?"

"Since we last met, what changes have happened that have been helpful?"

These questions assume positive change and encourage the counselee to search for and consider its implications.

WHEN THINGS ARE BETTER

If after asking about *helpful changes* the counselee reports positive change in regard to his described goal, the counselor will then highlight, support, and consolidate this change. When the counselor is *highlighting* changes, he is asking for more detail. Some questions that highlight change are these:

"Is it different when you do that?"

"What would your friends and family say is better?"

"That's an interesting idea. What made you think of that?"

"How did you do that?"

"When did this happen?"

"What happened that helped?"

"How did you know that was the right thing to do?"

To *support* these changes, that is, to help the counselee see them as meaningful, the counselor encourages him to describe the changes. Remember to maintain *fit*, and to reinforce the description with ongoing encouraging feedback. Any mention of change can be highlighted by the counselor's raised tone of voice, excited expressions such as "Super!" or "Hey, that's great!" or "Wow!" along with nonverbal positive gestures such as raising eyebrows or briefly leaning forward.

Along with these gestures, he may choose to interrupt when positive change is mentioned by using questions such as:

"What was that you just said?"

"Now, hold on a second. You did what?"

"Did you know that this was something you were able to do?"

"What is it about you that helped you to be able to do this?"

To *consolidate* these positive changes, the use of consolidating questions (O'Hanlon & Weiner-Davis, 1989) can be helpful. For example:

"What will you have to continue to do to get that to happen more often?"

"What will you have to do to prevent a backslide?"

"If we could see a couple of months into the future, what other changes will we notice?"

"What will you be doing if you get off track?"

"What will you be doing to remain on track?"

"What would you have to do to go backwards?"

Always be ready to discover more change. Once the counselor has developed, supported, and consolidated a change, he can start again by asking:

"What *other changes* have been helpful?"

"*What else* is better since the last time we met?"

After having explored as many changes as possible, the counselor can end a second session and subsequent sessions also with a break to develop supportive feedback. The same guidelines as in the first interview apply, and if the counselee is going to return, the counselor assigns the same observational task. Since the task has been effective, we continue to use something similar to what is already working.

If the counselee feels he will not need to come back for any other sessions, the counselor should make himself available and mention that he can return for a checkup at a later date.

Follow-up is essential to continue the process of consolidating gains. Follow-up should include Christian-education classes, church attendance, supportive fellowship, men's or women's group involvement, one-on-one discipleship when possible, and at least two follow-up phone calls *from the church counselor* over the next six months. Keep in mind the importance of confidentiality. Speak only to the counselee, and if you have to leave a message, maintain confidentiality.

WHEN THINGS ARE THE SAME

Again, the way this information has been arrived at is through *assuming positive change that has been helpful* since the last meeting. This will usually result in a report of no change, a shrug, or perhaps even silence. The counselee does not recognize anything as having changed for the better. This does not mean that there has not been any positive change, just that none stands out. I assume that God is active, and therefore I go into my detective mode, looking for the writing of the Spirit.

Before the counselor can highlight, support, and consolidate change, he will need to unearth an incidence of a strength or positive exception. Here the track options can be used as in the first interview. If you will envision the track options for a moment, the first is *recent change*. Some questions that will help discover any recent exceptions are these:

"Was there at least one good day since we last met?"

"What was your best day?"

"What was the best part of that day?"

If exceptions are reported, the counselor can then highlight, support, and consolidate that change. If no change is reported, a variation of the future-focus question can be asked. Again, if the counselee is unable to picture his life without the problem, the counselor uses the managing track. If this is unsuccessful, he can use the externalizing track. Again, if this track is unsuccessful, he can use the self-interest track. Each track leads back to clarifying the vision and consolidating gains.

If none of the track options are effective, the counselor should assess his own approach. Just as the counselee can get stuck and will need to begin moving forward, so also the counselor can get stuck and must then reexamine his approach. Perhaps the goal description is too vague. Is the vision of the outcome so large that the counselee cannot get a handle on what to do first? Remember, small change leads to larger change. The vision may be a "10," but the counselee needs only to try to move from, say, a "3" to a "4," not from a "3" to a "10." What specifically will that "4" look like? How will the counselee be doing it?

Remember, a goal description uses questions that create a hopeful depiction, seek specificity, describe action, empower, and create a track. Perhaps the part of the solution chosen was not the one the counselee really cared about.

WHEN THINGS HAVE BECOME WORSE

Once again, I begin the session asking about *helpful changes* that have occurred since the last meeting. In some cases the silence may very well be deafening. Not only does the counselee not recognize anything as having changed for the better, but things have become worse. Nevertheless, I will continue to assume that God is at work in his life and that exceptions can be discovered.

Before being able to highlight, support, and consolidate change, the counselor will need to address this negative response. The counselor may wish to move directly to the *managing track:*

"How have you managed?"

"What are you doing to manage when things are so bad?"

"How have you managed to do that?"

"How has that been helpful to you?"

"What would be a sign that things are getting a little better?"

"What would it take to make that happen?"

If the counselor is unable to create a solution description through the managing track, he may wish to try externalizing the problem. As before, it is possible that the goal description is too vague. If the vision of the outcome is too large, the counselee will not be able to get a clear picture of what to do next. Again, remember that specifics are important. Small change leads to larger change.

If an exception or strength is identified, continue with supportive feedback, clarifying the goal. This session should be treated like the first interview, with a *different* task given. Let the task be mutually agreed upon. You could even give the counselee a choice of tasks.

WHEN THERE HAS BEEN A SETBACK

After counseling has been concluded, the counselor may discover during a follow-up call that there has been a setback; the counselee has gotten off track. After encouraging him to come in for a checkup, the following questions could be asked:

"What will you have to do to get back on track?"

"What have you learned from getting off track?"

"Even though you got off track, has anything been better?"

"How have you been able to manage in the face of these setbacks?"

"What will you have to do to stay on track?"

"How will you get that to happen?"

"What else will need to happen?"

At the close of the session the counselor should prepare supportive feedback as usual, *normalizing* the setback and consolidating gains. He should retain an expectant, hopeful, and confident attitude, viewing the setback as "two steps forward, one step backward."

BOB AND ALICE, SESSION TWO

In chapter 12, in the section titled "Goal Description," you may recall I referred to a married couple named Bob and Alice. They had been married for one year. Bob was undecided about a job he had been offered in the area because Alice wanted to return to Cleveland, where her family lived. This had become a conflict and was now affecting their marriage. When I asked how this was happening, Alice began to weep.

It turned out that the issue was actually Alice's lack of personal independence, not her desire to return to Cleveland. Moving back home was a means to an end. When we proceeded directly to the end, which turned out to be promoting independence, the goal of independence was clarified for her. Her solution included taking responsibility for herself and not "beating herself" up so much. This goal was further described.

Alice was asked to imagine a track to her future on a scale of 1 to 10. Ten is feeling no longer isolated and living and acting more independently; 1 is how bad things were when she and her husband called for an appointment. She said she was at about a 3. She was asked how she had gone from a 1 to a 3 after calling for an appointment. Her response was that she felt more confident about what she had to do next.

After the break she was asked whether continuing to do these things would put her on the beginning of a track to getting what she hoped for when she came in to see me. She said they would, and the goal then became the continuation of these changes. Her personal goal was to move from a 3 to a 4, and both Bob and Alice were asked to specifically observe when Alice was "doing a 4 or above." When she arrived at that point, they were to simply make a mental note of what was different when it happened—not only for Alice, but also for Bob and other relationships. Whatever was working she was to do more of and to observe what happened when she did.

Bob and Alice returned for a second appointment. After they were seated, I asked them, "Since we last met, what changes have happened that have been helpful?" *Notice, I did not ask about the task. If they had done it, this would become evident. If they had not, little is gained by asking them why they had not.*

"Well," Alice replied with a smile, "actually quite a lot. Bob helped me get my driver's permit and is now giving me driving lessons."

"Wait a second now. You did what?" I replied enthusiastically, sitting abruptly forward to *support* this change as meaningful. To *highlight* this change, that is, to look for details, I asked, "When did this happen?"

"It was only a couple of days after our meeting," Alice answered.

"Well, tell me . . . how did you do that?" I asked.

Again, Alice spoke up. "Bob drove me in to get my permit and has been helping me study for the driver's test. We go out every evening to practice driving too. I'm doing pretty good, aren't I, honey?"

"Oh yea, she's a natural," Bob replied with a smirk. Alice gave him an elbow in the side. Clearly they were both enjoying this.

Entering into this fun exchange and wanting to *support* it, I said, "That's terrific, a natural! Well, that's because you have such a great instructor, right Alice?"

"Bob's been very patient with me," she replied with a grin.

It was evident that they had enjoyed a good week together. Again, wanting to *highlight* this change, I asked, "Is it different when you do that? You know, the way you have been working on this together?"

Now Bob spoke up. "To tell you the truth, I had been avoiding it. I didn't realize it was so important to Alice. Now that we've started, we've been doing pretty well. I thought we were going to die a couple of times"—another poke in the side from Alice—"but all in all it's been fun to spend the time together doing this."

I took a second to jot down a note regarding husbands and wives spending time together and then asked, "Bob, how did you know that was the right thing to do?"

"I guess I just started seeing how much Alice needed to be able to get around on her own," Bob replied thoughtfully. "You know, I traded in the car and bought one with an automatic transmission."

"What!" I exclaimed, nearly jumping out of my seat. Both Bob and Alice started laughing at my reaction. "That's terrific," I added. So you really made a decision to help your wife. Wow, that's really great. Tell me, would your family or friends say anything is better between the two of you this week?"

"I know my mom would," Alice quickly replied. "I had been crying on the phone with her so often. Our last phone call was real different. You know, I'm just so excited about finally driving that, well, we just had a real good talk. I know I enjoyed it more!"

At this point I asked about changes Bob had noticed about himself since our last meeting. He was enthusiastic about the change in what he called the "attitude" at home. I continued to ask for details, highlighting and supporting change, and asking what else had been different. After exploring these changes, I wanted to *consolidate* them. I asked, "If we could see a couple of months into the future, what other changes will we notice?" (Notice I did not say "would we notice.")

After thinking a moment, Alice replied with a smile, "Well, I'll have a good job. We will have more money, and we'll be able to go out more." Bob was nodding his head in agreement.

"This may sound like an unusual question," I asked carefully, "but I wonder, what would you have to do to go backwards?"

Bob was the first to reply. "All I would have to do is start to ignore Alice's needs again."

Alice went on to say, "I guess I would just start sitting around the house feeling sorry for myself again."

I was impressed with the clarity of their vision. "So what will you need to do to remain on track?" I wondered.

"I guess we'll need to keep doing what we've been doing," Bob replied. "Alice will need to find that job, and I can't complain about having a little more money. I think we both have enjoyed spending more time together." Alice nodded her head in agreement. "We'll need to keep looking for those things that are working, like you told us to," Bob continued. "I know I'll need to remember to help Alice feel more self-reliant."

At this, Alice added, "And I'll need to act more self-reliant too."

We took a few more minutes to describe what Alice is doing when she *is* more self-reliant, and then we took a break. (The break was agreed upon before the discussion began.)

After the break I returned with *supportive feedback:*

"I'm very impressed with your efforts to look for what is working and to deliberately try to do more of that. It is clear to me that you both care a great deal about each other. Bob, you have really gone out of your way to help Alice learn to drive and ultimately to get a job. And Alice, you have made a clear decision to get in gear and go forward, both for yourself and for your husband. You are working well together and serving one another. It seems to me that both of you are reaping the benefits of obedience to the Lord.

"Consider that it was the apostle Paul who encouraged husbands and wives to submit to one another out of reverence to God (Eph. 5:21). That means that we must put our spouse first, and that's what you have both been doing.

"I'm also reminded of an article I read that revealed that husbands and wives who are best friends have a higher percentage of overall happiness than husbands and wives who are not best friends. That is, the friendship of marriage spilled over into the rest of their lives. I believe you will both continue to discover that as your friendship grows, so also will your overall satisfaction in other areas of life.

"I am impressed with how well you relate to each other as friends—the way you can relax with one another and kid each other without being offended. What I would like to suggest is that you continue to do what you have been doing. It seems obvious to me that you are both on track. You may wish to take notice of what you are doing when you are being best friends. Intentionally do more of that; it's clearly working. Don't forget to observe what happens around you when you do this and how you react to one another when you are acting like best friends.

"I would also like you to give serious thought to attending our couples' class on Sunday mornings. They are getting into some information that goes right along with what you have been doing. Plus, you will have fellowship with other young couples like yourselves. Now is the time to go forward with the Lord. You have been trusting Him, and He has been blessing you, but it seems to me that you are ready to go forward now, more so than you were just a short time ago."

Later Bob and Alice often paused after Sunday services, just to let me know they were doing okay. I also followed up with personal calls during the next six months, and they continued to report that things were going well, and they were still on track.

In review, in the second and subsequent sessions the counselor will be asking about changes that have been helpful; highlighting these changes by asking for details; supporting change as meaningful; consolidating these changes; and then starting over, asking what other changes have been helpful. ■

CHAPTER FIFTEEN

Bringing It All Together: A Case Example

Knowing what to ignore has become one of my most important counseling skills. . . . If counselors do not work to promote change early in the process—if they convey to clients a belief that nothing substantial will occur for a long time—they will more often than not be proven correct. ▪ *Charles Huber and Barbara Backlund, 1993, pp. 121, 125*

As an example of how I arrange for the counseling interview and possible subsequent sessions, I have chosen the complex issue of sexual abuse. Some of the more frequent issues church counselors encounter—depression, anxiety, marital problems, and family concerns—have already been considered in this book through the numerous case illustrations. Sexual abuse qualifies as a topic that many church counselors shy away from, quickly referring the counselee to experts. But to do so implies to the counselee that his problem is too complicated. His problem must be very serious indeed to be so quickly referred to a professional.

Although there most certainly is a time to refer, as well as use adjunct services, referral should not be made out of fear that the problem is simply too complex. No matter how difficult the problem, the counselee still has strengths that can be directed toward solutions.

SFPC ASSUMPTIONS APPLIED

How do the nine assumptions that inform SFPC empower us in helping those who have been sexually abused? Let us review each assumption through the lens of sexual abuse.*

1. God is already active in the counselee.
2. Complex problems do not demand complex solutions.
3. Finding exceptions helps create solutions.
4. The counselee is always changing.
5. The counselee is the expert and defines goals.
6. Solutions are cocreated.
7. The counselee is not the problem, the problem is.
8. The counseling relationship is positional.
9. The counselor's focus is on solutions.

1. God Is Already Active in the Counselee

Do we trust what God has been doing in the counselee, even when sexual abuse is reported? When we do, we begin to look for evidence of His love and preparation. Deficiency language presupposes a world of victimization. The language of faith and trust presupposes strengths, hope, positive change, and the successful completion of counseling. All counseling language should suggest this hope.

A counselee's unique identity is being cocreated by the Spirit and oneself. This identity cannot be purposefully formed by human intervention. It can only be assisted. The goal of counseling is not to help the counselee "work through his or her abuse." Rather, it is to stand alongside the counselee and support him as he seeks to incorporate all of life's experience and to move forward in Christ.

2. Complex Problems Do Not Demand Complex Solutions

The problem does not need to be clearly defined for effective counseling to take place. Often it cannot be clearly defined. Rather, it is the solution that needs to be clearly defined. Complicated problems such as childhood sexual abuse need not require complicated solu-

*I am deeply indebted to Michael Durrant for his personal instruction at the East Coast Solution-Focused Brief Therapy Conference regarding sexual abuse and solution-focused counseling.

tions. Instead, look for evidences that the Spirit has already placed in the counselee's life—clues to ways of getting unstuck.

3. Finding Exceptions Helps Create Solutions

When viewing 100 percent of a person's past, we discover that the problems that are now holding him back were not always present. What are the exceptions to the problems? What was happening instead? Finding these exceptions reveals the counselee's strengths and capabilities. Sexual abuse often alters the counselee's view of himself, overwhelming the present moment, and hindering utilization of these strengths.

4. The Counselee Is Always Changing

The sexually abused counselee has been changing and will continue to change. Change is unavoidable. It is so much a part of life that the counselee cannot keep himself from changing. But this change must be viewed as meaningful and within the counselee's control. Thus the counselee will need to view himself as "in agreement" with the work of the Spirit (Amos 3:3), rather than struggling alone; in control, rather than out of control; capable and victorious, rather than incompetent; and being considerate and loving with himself, rather than suffering self-blame and self-hate. Just as a *rising tide lifts all the ships in a harbor*, so also increasing personal control and competence creates new ways of perceiving past struggles and fears.

5. The Counselee Is the Expert and Defines Goals

In the area of childhood sexual abuse there are so many experts that the counselee's goals may not be given proper attention. Yet the counselee *is the expert* on his or her life. Instead of gaining competence and control, the counselee turns over control to an expert who may strongly encourage a retelling of the abuse. This may actually disempower the counselee. The counselor needs to put the *counselee* in control.

6. Solutions Are Cocreated

In the construction of an individual perception of reality, the counselor cocreates with the counselee a personal world where there is an opportunity for positive change. Focusing on a reality in which the problem does not exist is of greater assistance to the counselee than focusing on the past with the problem.

7. The Counselee Is Not the Problem, the Problem Is

Sexual abuse is often so overwhelming that it may be more helpful to consider the *impact* of the abuse. Creating a clear description of a positive outcome is easier when focusing on the impact and effects of the abuse rather than on the abuse itself. It is often more helpful to consider what gets in the way of the client's finding or noticing solutions than working through the sexual abuse.

8. The Counseling Relationship Is Positional

A willing position is more readily gained through a focus on a personal goal. Remaining in a blaming position weakens the counselee, resulting in his inability to view himself as part of the solution. Thus, assisting the counselee to gain a clear vision of a solution will prompt him to move forward toward a healthier outcome.

9. The Counselor's Focus Is on Solutions

Staying focused on the counselee's personal control is essential when counseling those who have been sexually abused. Although the counselee will continue to have disturbing and often painful memories, he still has capabilities and strengths with which to create solutions. Remember, if a suggested solution is not working, stop doing it and try something different. Do more of what is working.

CHILDHOOD SEXUAL ABUSE—A NARRATIVE

Carolyn had been growing more and more despondent lately. Her relationship with her five-year-old daughter was suffering, and her work performance was down. She felt as if she were carrying an emotional burden that was getting too difficult to bear. Two of her friends, noticing her change, wondered if there was anything they could do. Since they worked together and also attended the same church, they convinced her to talk with their pastor. The pastor referred her to me.

Carolyn walked into the room accompanied by her friends, all three accompanied by a cloud of doom. At first I did not know which was Carolyn. All three found seats, with Carolyn sitting farthest away. They were obviously readying themselves for what they anticipated was going to be a serious and difficult conversation.

"What brings you all in to see me today?" I began.

Carolyn's friends responded by explaining how depressed she had been and how concerned they were about her. I listened carefully to their concerns as Carolyn remained silent, looking sadly at the floor.

"I think Carolyn is indeed blessed to have such good friends," I said. "It is clear to me how much you both care about her. If it is all right with everyone, I would like to speak with Carolyn alone for a moment. When we're done, we'll take a short break to collect our thoughts, and I'll prepare some feedback for everyone. Afterward, I'll be calling you back in to enlist your support regarding whatever Carolyn chooses to do." Everyone agreed, and as her friends left, I moved over across from Carolyn and prepared to listen to her story. I asked her if it would be all right if I jotted down some thoughts that I might wish to bring up later to talk about, and she said yes.

Trying to match the seriousness of her mood, I leaned toward her and asked, "So what is it your friends wanted us to talk about today?" (*encouraging movement from an attendee position to a willing position*).

At first Carolyn would not raise her eyes to look at me. She seemed very nervous and hesitant.

"Well, they know I've been real stressed out at work lately," she replied. "I've received new responsibilities, and I guess I'm not handling the pressure very well."

As I listened, Carolyn began to tell me about her job. She had responsibility for employees who were unresponsive to her wishes. Her boss had asked all his managers to concentrate specifically on what is not working and to bring these deficiencies to the attention of all concerned on a regular basis. (A real prescription for trouble!) Thus her job had become nearly unmanageable.

She had also been feeling very sad lately, and after working hours she had been staying in her apartment most of the time. As she had become more withdrawn, her insecurity had increased in all of her relationships. She also implied that she felt ashamed and worthless. During this time I offered verbal and nonverbal support as she told her story, *being with her* in it. Yet I still had not been invited in. Once she started, she barely stopped to take a breath.

It also seemed that there was more she wanted to tell me, and I did not want to move too quickly, inadvertently guiding the conversation away from her true concern.

As Carolyn continued, she grew more comfortable with me. Initial trust was being established, and she now looked up and began to speak to me more directly. She mentioned having some disturbing dreams lately that have been making her nervous and unhappy.

"In these dreams," she said slowly, "I'm a little girl again, and my uncle is with me. He . . . he molested me." Her tears began to flow.

At this point an alarm went off within me. I was tempted to lapse into deficiency conversation and victimization. I could encourage a discussion of repressed memories, family secrets, and denial. Carolyn had presented a view of herself as a victim and her family as abusive. I could reinforce this belief by focusing on it further, or I could look beyond the abuse and trust in her strengths and God's sovereign intention.

In order to *offer control* of the conversation to Carolyn I said, "Some people who have been treated in this way believe it helps them to talk about what happened. Sometimes they have never told anyone before, and they need to bring this awful memory out into the open. Others would rather get on with their lives, not feeling it is necessary to discuss the abusive treatment they received. What would you like to do? What do you believe will be most helpful?" (Durrant, 1995, p. 7).

She decided to talk for a while about what had happened but did not get very specific. I gave her time to finish this painful part of the story. Her uncle had sexually abused her for two years from the time she was eight years old. Her uncle died when she was ten, and she had not been disturbed by the memory of the abuse until the dreams began. She tried to discuss this with her mother but unfortunately received little support.

She paused, then said, "I just don't know why I'm experiencing this now. Have you ever heard of this happening to someone?" By this she meant her dreams. (*This is also an invitation.*)

Giving a brief educative comment at the onset, I replied, "There is much we do not understand about dreams. I believe that most dreams reveal random thoughts; it's the brain's attempt to sort itself out, so to speak. I know that if we don't dream we can become physically ill, even hallucinating when we're awake. I also believe that sad and unhappy memories evoke sad and unhappy feelings, just as joyful and happy memories evoke joyful and happy feelings." I said this to remove some of the fear and to *normalize* the dream experience. "These are very sad memories for you, and of course they can cause sad feelings as well.

"I wonder . . . many times between calling for an appointment and the first counseling session, people already notice that something seems a little better. Have you noticed anything since you first thought of talking to the pastor, and now to me?" (*seeking clues for recent-change track*).

"I really can't think of anything," Carolyn replied. "I've just been so down lately. Like you said, these memories have been having a big effect on me."

"Carolyn, let's step out on faith and say that our time together has been helpful to you. How will you know it has been helpful?" I asked (*future-focus track*).

"Well," Carolyn said thoughtfully, "I know I won't feel so depressed all the time."

"What will you be doing instead?" I wondered (*creating a hopeful depiction—i.e., focusing on the presence of something rather than the absence of something*).

Looking up into my eyes, she replied, "I think . . . I'll just have a good day. I'll be happier."

"Well, let's look at your good day and see what will be different when you're happier. If I could watch this day on video, what would be the first thing I would see that is different?" I asked carefully.

Carolyn thought for a moment and said, "I think I would wake up and spend some time with the Lord. I haven't been doing that lately."

"What will be happening next?" I asked.

"I would go in to Shanna, my daughter, and wake her up. Recently, I've just been calling in and telling her to get up."

"How will you be waking her up on this good day?" I asked (*clarifying the initial vision by describing personal action*).

"I would go in and sit next to her in bed," Carolyn said, now smiling. "I'd be stroking her hair, maybe even scratching her back. I've been so abrupt with her lately, I know it's affected her."

"Hey, that's a great idea! Boy, I know I like getting my back scratched in the morning. It can make me look at the whole day differently," I said, also smiling. "What else would you be doing specifically?" I asked (*seeking specificity*).

"Well, I'd be helping her get her clothes sorted out—you know, just spending time with her."

As I continued to ask "what else" kinds of questions, Carolyn described for me the rest of her "good" morning with Shanna. Instead of eating quickly with her daughter, she would be spending more time at breakfast and also including her in devotions. Instead of simply driving over to the baby-sitter in silence, they would be talking and even singing children's hymns. Instead of hastily dropping her off at the baby-sitter's home, she would be walking her up to the door, holding her hand, and hugging and kissing her good-bye. These are things she used to do but had stopped doing.

"Has your relationship with Shanna been improved since you stopped doing these things?" I asked with a smile. Of course the answer was no. I briefly mentioned the guideline of "If it's not working, stop doing it and try something different . . . then do more of what works."

"So what will be different at work on this good day?" I asked.

"The attitude at the shop would be a lot better. There wouldn't be so much tension all the time. I wouldn't hate going to work."

"What will your co-workers see you doing that is different?" I wondered.

"Well, I would be looking for ways to compliment instead of looking for what they're doing wrong. I know I might take a little flak from my supervisor for that, but I think it would help in the long run."

"Are there times when you do a little of this now?" I wondered (*seeking exceptions*).

"Well, I used to try looking for the best in those who work with me and for me. I still do, but not as often anymore."

"What was different about the times when you did look for ways to compliment your fellow workers?" I asked.

"Usually, work was more enjoyable. It just made the job go more smoothly."

"What will have to happen for you to begin to do it that way again?" I asked.

"I think I just need to do it," Carolyn answered deliberately.

Carolyn continued to describe the rest of her day at work as I encouraged her and asked her "what else" questions. Instead of staying quiet and swallowing her frustration, she would be talking to her co-workers and smiling at them. Instead of avoiding the main office, she would be going in with a smile and a professional presence. Instead of bringing her work home with her, she would be leaving as much of it as possible at the office. Instead of closing herself off, she would be opening up a little more.

"Well, now you're leaving the office," I said. "What do I see next on the video? What else is happening on this good day?"

"I used to go in and talk with my baby-sitter for awhile," she replied thoughtfully. "Recently, I've been picking up my daughter and leaving right away."

"What will your baby-sitter notice about you on this good day?"

"I think I'll be going in and sitting with her for a few minutes . . . you know, ask her how her day has been. She will notice that I'm also concerned about her and about how Shanna was all day."

Through my continued use of solution-focused questions, Carolyn went on to describe in some detail her ride home with her daughter, their dinner together, bedtime, and her own quiet time after Shanna was in bed. "Is there anything else about this good day that is different?" I asked.

"I think I'd also be planning to get out with my friends at church from time to time. I know Joyce [the baby-sitter] would watch Shanna. I believe I'd be getting out of the house more. I'd be back in church more often too."

"I think that's a great idea!" I said while leaning toward her. "Well, we've talked about a great many differences. I'd like to take our short break at this point to reflect on what we have been discussing. While I'm out of the office you may wish to think of any thoughts or questions you may have for me. When I return, I'll have some feedback and suggestions. After we discuss this feedback I'll invite your friends back in. Is this all right with you?" She agreed.

When I returned a few minutes later I began by saying:

"I am very impressed by the openness you have shown today, (*encouraging positive action*). It took real courage to talk about your dreams of when your uncle molested you, and the effect they are having on you today (*reducing fears*). It is also evident to me that you deeply love your daughter. It is so difficult to be a single parent, and you are clearly working very hard to balance the job with your responsibilities to Shanna (*fortifying strengths*). I'm also impressed by your desire to look for the best in others. If more people acted this way, our world would be a much more enjoyable place to live in.

"Let me take a moment to remind you that the feelings associated with the memory of the sexual abuse from your uncle are characteristic of that memory (*normalizing*). Bad memories tend to result in bad feelings. The writer of Proverbs encouraged us to trust in the Lord with all our hearts and not lean on our own understanding. Instead we should acknowledge Christ in all we do. Then our paths are made straight by the Holy Spirit.

"As terrible as the feelings are that come from such memories, God encourages us not to lean on our own understanding of our memories of the past, or even our present or future concerns. That is, we cannot see the whole picture. We may not now understand how He can incorporate even such horrible memories into our lives to help us grow and mature, but this is His intention. Perhaps your experiences will ultimately cause you to be more sensitive to others who have also been hurt—they probably have already.

"I think this is what Paul meant when he wrote in Second Corinthians 1:3–4: 'Praise be to the God and Father of our Lord Jesus Christ, the Father of compassion and the God of all comfort, who comforts us in all our troubles, so that we can comfort those in any trouble with the comfort we ourselves have received by God.' You may wish to bring this awful memory back up at a later time for us to discuss—considering it from the perspective of who you are today (*educative comments*).

"Now you have described in very specific terms what a good day would look like (*reviewing the goal description*). You have said, quite clearly, what you will be doing with your daughter and how you will be spending more time with her in the morning. You will be sitting with her in bed in the morning, scratching her back—I liked that scratching the back part!—and guiding her more closely through the day. At work you will be more positive, talking more with your co-workers and smiling at them. Instead of avoiding your central office, you'll be going in with a smile, staying professional even if they don't.

"You also said you will be taking a greater interest in your babysitter again, asking her about her day. You mentioned getting out with your friends for a special evening, which I think is a great idea, and also going to church more often.

"Now I'd like to ask you a question: On a scale of 1 to 10, with 10 meaning you will do anything to solve the problem that brought you in to see me today, and 1 being you will sit and wait for something to happen, where would you say you are today?"

"I think I'm at a 10," Carolyn replied without hesitation. "I don't want to keep feeling so depressed."

"All right then, I'd like you to imagine for a moment a track," I said while pointing toward the far wall (*creating a track*). "Now imagine that the end of the track is a 10. The 10 represents your good day with everything you envisioned happening, everything you have described to me, and 1 represents how bad things were when you made this appointment to come to see me. Where would you say you are on that track now?"

"I'm afraid I'm not very high . . . probably about a 2," Carolyn replied sheepishly.

"Now wait a minute! How did you move from a 1 to a 2?" I asked, sitting forward.

"I guess, just having a plan helps. I . . . I feel a little better since we talked."

"I'm glad. What would have to happen to move to a 3?" I wondered.

"Not a lot. Perhaps just spending more time with my daughter in the morning. I think I could get further down the track than that. I think I could get to a 6!" she said confidently.

"All right, here is what I'd like you to do between now and the next time we talk together," I said. "I would like you to do a small piece of your good day, between a 3 and a 6 on the track, and look for what helps when you do so. Whatever is helpful, do more of it on purpose. Also, I want you to notice what takes place when you do this. What is different with your daughter, co-workers, baby-sitter, friends . . . whoever. I'm wondering if there will be any reaction from them and I'd like you to consciously look for it. Will you do this?"

"Yes, I will," she agreed.

"As you continue to do these things, would you see yourself as being on track to getting what you wanted when you came to see me today?"

"Yes, I do. Very much so!" Carolyn replied thoughtfully.

"Before I call your friends back into the office," I said, "let me say that it must have taken exceptional strength and courage to have told me things that you have never told anyone else but your mother. Having done this, how do you think it will make a difference for you this week; and would it be helpful for you to continue to talk about what happened to you with others who have had similar experiences?"

"I'm glad I talked about it with you today," Carolyn replied reflectively. "I don't know that I need to talk about it with anyone else right now. Perhaps I'll want to later. It still bothers me that my mom won't talk with me about it. But I feel like I'm ready to move on with what I can do to make a difference."

Before I called in her friends, I gave Carolyn some information I had on a Christian support group for women who had been sexually abused as children. Then I invited her friends to join us.

"It is clear to me that you are both good friends to Carolyn," I said after they were seated. "Carolyn and I have discussed a number of things this morning. What I would like you to do is consciously take note of Carolyn's actions this week. I want you to look for things that Carolyn is doing that you feel are helpful. I would also like you to be prepared to observe changes, even minor ones. You don't need to discuss what you notice, but come back with Carolyn if you can and tell me what you noticed, if anything." They both agreed.

SESSION TWO

"Since we last met," I asked Carolyn and her friends, "what changes have happened that have been helpful?" (*assuming positive change that has been helpful*). All of their moods were more confident than the previous week. My question was directed more at her friends though, and they responded first.

"I've noticed a difference," said one. The other was nodding in agreement. "At work Carolyn has been more outgoing with everyone. I wanted to say something to her about it but I didn't, since you told us to wait and tell you."

"She's been much more . . . together," said her other friend carefully. "More like her old self."

After speaking a few moments more and thanking them, I asked Carolyn's friends to step out for a while so I could discuss these observations, and any other changes, alone with Carolyn. They agreed.

"So, what *is* better since the last time we got together?" I asked conspiratorially. "What about these changes your friends observed?"

"Well, I think I've definitely gotten to a 6! Maybe even better!" Carolyn exclaimed.

"Really," I said, matching her enthusiasm. "What happened that helped?" (*highlighting the change by asking for details*)

"Well, it really began with my time with Shanna," Carolyn explained. "Our first morning after talking with you was so blessed. She was so thirsty for our relationship, and I guess I was too. We spent time together every morning. I scratched her back and brushed her hair, all the little things that I had stopped doing. We sang on the way to Joyce's house (the baby-sitter) and I walked her to the door, and her hug was just so . . . terrific.

"By the time I got to work, I was feeling pretty good. Somehow, it wasn't that hard to smile at work. On Wednesday I decided to talk to my supervisor about the policy of looking for things that are wrong at work. We had a really good talk. I can see now that Mr. Jackson, that's our boss, has been putting him under a lot of pressure lately. But he liked what I had to say about looking for what's working and told me to go ahead but to also fix what's not working."

"How did you know that was the right thing to do?" I asked excitedly (*wanting to further highlight this change*).

"Well, it struck me that it was a lot like what we were doing in counseling. I figured, well you know . . . what was happening at work wasn't helping," she said. "It was just time to try something different."

"Did you know that this was something you were able to do?" I asked (*supporting this change as meaningful*). "I mean, what is it about you that enabled you to do this?"

"I think I was able to do this . . . because . . . I was feeling good about myself," Carolyn replied slowly. "I just felt confident. I knew what I wanted to do. And . . . I wanted to stay on track."

"You did what? You wanted to stay on track! Is that what you just said," I responded with *supportive* overexaggeration. Carolyn began to laugh, and I reached over and gave her a high five.

"So tell me," I said to *consolidate* this remarkable change, "what will you need to be doing to remain on track at work?"

"I think as long as I'm okay with Shanna and feel good about myself, I'll be doing all right at work. I know I need to keep talking with my supervisor. I discovered something about his life when we finally talked, and I want to keep him in prayer and try to help him a little too."

"That's terrific," I agreed. "I will also support him in prayer. So tell me, *what else is better* since the last time we met?"

Carolyn went on to describe other changes that had taken place since our first meeting. She was quite true to her commitment to "be a 6." She had spent time with her baby-sitter and with her friends. She had even volunteered to help out in the nursery at her church. I continued to *highlight*, *support*, and *consolidate* these changes as well. Finally I asked,

"What have you noticed that is different when you are doing these things? What have you noticed about how you feel and about how others are responding to you?"

"Well, I am feeling quite a bit better. I was so down in the dumps that any positive change would be noticeable. I really am feeling better. I did have some more dreams, but when I woke up I went right into Shanna's room and began to stroke her hair. I realized that I didn't have to let the memory of what my uncle did keep affecting me the way it was." (It was gratifying to see that Carolyn was now considering the *impact* of the sexual abuse from within her own competence.)

"I've noticed the biggest difference in Shanna. She is much happier now that we're talking again. I think Ann and Linda [her two friends] noticed some difference too."

"I wonder, if we could see a couple of months into the future, what other changes will you notice?" I asked (*consolidating change*).

"I think we will see more of the same. I want to spend more time with Shanna. I also am getting more involved at church. I would like to help more at work, but I'll have to move slowly there. Linda and Ann have mentioned going out next weekend. Lately, I've been saying no, but this time I'm going to go. I think we'll just be going out to dinner, but it will give us some time to talk."

"So what will you be doing to remain on track this week?" I asked with a smile.

"Just keep living good days," Carolyn replied firmly.

"I'd like to take our short break at this point to reflect on what we have been discussing," I said. "Again, while I'm out of the office you may wish to consider any thoughts or questions you may have for me. When I return, I'll have some feedback and suggestions. After we discuss this feedback I'll invite you're friends back in. Okay?" She agreed.

When I returned, I began by saying, "I am very impressed by the obvious determination you have shown toward last week's discussion. Your efforts with your daughter and at work have been terrific" (*encouraging positive action*). "You should be very proud of yourself. I'm also impressed by the courage you have shown at work. Taking the first step in communicating with your supervisor took a lot of strength and faith (*fortifying strengths*).

"I think faith is involved because you are trusting God that when you reach out to someone, even if you work for him, God will support your action. You have put forth a great effort this past week. Change is often hard, but you have approached it with persistence (*educative comment*).

"You mentioned that you are now getting more involved at church. I think helping out will be greatly appreciated. I know you also want to improve your work environment. I agree that you should move slowly but faithfully, trusting God to open doors for you as you seek to support and encourage your co-workers. I think going out with Linda and Ann for dinner to talk is a great idea too (*reviewing goal description*). As you continue to do these things, will you feel you are still on track to getting what you were hoping for when we first talked last week?"

"Absolutely," Carolyn replied, nodding her head thoughtfully.

"All right," I replied. "Last week I asked you to do a small piece of the good day, between a 3 and a 6 on the track, and look for what helps when you do so. Why don't you continue to do this, perhaps looking for a 6 or 7. Remember that whatever is helpful, do more of it on purpose. Also, keep in mind that I want you to continue to notice what takes place when you do this. Okay?" (*simple del/ob task*). Carolyn agreed. The issue of a support group did not come up, and I decided to leave attendance up to Carolyn. I invited her friends in and thanked them for their help and support.

An appointment was scheduled for two weeks later. Carolyn called before the appointment and expressed satisfaction with her progress at this time. She was still trying to open a more honest dialogue with her mother, but other than that, things continued to go well. I called a few times over the next six months and Carolyn was always happy to hear from me and gave a positive report on her progress. I remained available if further assistance was required. ■

CHAPTER SIXTEEN

Questions and Answers: Some Final Considerations

- What about emotions, how are they addressed?
- What about psychotropic medications?
- How about personality disorders?
- What about psychotic and schizophrenic disorders?
- What about dissociative identity disorders?

I have been asked whether a solution-focused approach simply glosses over the really difficult problems. How does a solution-focused approach address these questions? Well, let us look at the first two questions together:

1. WHAT ABOUT EMOTIONS? WHAT ABOUT PSYCHOTROPIC MEDICATIONS?

It is now believed that thoughts stimulate chemical hormones. For example, when boy meets girl and thoughts are full of new love, the body releases chemicals that are experienced as emotions. Acetylcholine produces a feeling of excitement. Dopamine induces a feeling of well-being. Norepinephrine induces feelings of pleasure, contentment, joy, and love. Serotonin maintains a generalized feeling of emotional security.

Much of modern psychiatry is a result of the discovery of these chemical hormones, or neurotransmitters. It is believed that a *decrease* in the level of serotonin or norepinephrine will result in feelings we label depression. But how does this decrease occur? It is a little like the question of the chicken and the egg. Which came first, thoughts that resulted in a lessening of these neurotransmitters or a lessening of the neurotransmitters resulting in thoughts of depression? Biochemical changes do occur in the brain in correlation with extreme changes in mood. But which occur first?

We do know that some hormones may produce depression. For example, Cushing's disease increases the output of steroids and produces depression in some cases. Hypothyroidism may also be identified with depression. Although there is a connection between these hormonal disorders and depression, it is still undetermined whether the depression is actually caused by the hormonal disorder (Breggin, 1991, p. 145).

Prozac (fluoxetine) tends to selectively affect the neurotransmitter serotonin and therefore to have a more limited impact on the brain, with fewer side effects. According to one psychiatrist these may be premature conclusions.

> Serotonin nerves spread throughout most of the brain—including the emotion-regulating limbic system and frontal lobes—and are thus involved in multiple functions that defy our current understanding or imagination. Prozac makes serotonin more available by inhibiting its removal from the synaptic region between nerves.
>
> *Breggin, 1991, p. 163*

This is called blocking re-uptake of the serotonin. Prozac, like any other medication, has possible side effects. For some users headaches, nausea, somnolence, anxiety, agitation, insomnia, bizarre dreams, loss of appetite, diarrhea, dry mouth, sweating, dizziness, impotence, inability to achieve orgasm, seizures, and rash are some of the possible side effects. Many of these go away after a couple of weeks. Yet Prozac can also cause hypoglycemia and on rare occasions a severe rash with fever, joint pain, and swollen lymph nodes. A "Prozac syndrome" may develop, including hot flashes and flushing, agitation, nausea, muscle tremors, and sweating.

How should psychopharmaceuticals fit into the practice of counseling? For most professional therapists, antidepressant medications such as Prozac, Paxil, Zoloft, and other psychotropic medications used for a variety of other emotional problems, are *the* initial therapeutic decision. Remember Carolyn from the preceding chapter? She reportedly was depressed. It turned out that she was having recurring dreams of the abuse she suffered in childhood.

The first course of action is to treat the depression. For many therapists and psychiatrists this means drug therapy. There is some wisdom in this approach since it takes from two to four weeks to receive any benefit from such a course of treatment. But while many of Carolyn's thoughts were linked to her past, others represented present stressful realities and even future fears. It is quite possible that her painful memories, combined with present challenges, *caused the decrease* in the level of serotonin or norepinephrine, resulting in feelings we now label depression.

That emotional dysfunction is primarily a *disease* of the brain has not been medically established. Even though such dysfunction has a "chemical" foundation, so do *all* emotions. There is far too much we do not yet understand about the brain. Although I may sound overly suspicious in saying this, remember that the pharmaceutical companies also have an immense financial investment in the *disease* concept—and the ability to influence therapy choices. Therefore, at this juncture I do not encourage drug therapy as automatically the only therapy choice for such individuals.

If thoughts, even memories, result in a decrease of neurotransmitters, which in turn result in emotional change, then a change of thinking becomes a legitimate choice for counseling. This can be approached through the cognitive change that results from a focus on solutions, as demonstrated in Carolyn's case. When medications are necessary, I encourage using both medications and counseling together. In this way the usefulness of the psychotropic medication is in providing the counselee with a *level playing field* for counseling to take place.

We are a new creation in Christ. In Christ there *is* cognitive transformation (Rom. 12:2). Now, how shall we live as a new creation? What will we be doing differently? Are there times when a small piece of that is happening now? As the outcome is envisioned, the track forward is clarified.

When even the smallest amount of progress forward along the track is noted, the counselee is empowered—his thinking and actions are more in harmony with the *intention* of the Spirit, and his emotions are altered. If the counselee is off track, his emotions can serve to act as a *warning light*. This, by the way, is a more legitimate purpose for focusing on feelings. He now knows when he has inadvertently gotten off track. *This reframes the meaning of the emotional distress.*

The counselee can now envision getting back on track, an outcome or solution that he can clearly visualize, step by step. Even small steps begin forward motion toward his goal. He is now thinking through his actions and acting his way into less distressing emotions. Increasing competence and mastery of life in Christ is the goal of SFPC.

A word of caution is in order here. If someone who is already on psychotropic medications enters into a counseling relationship with you, and if he perceives the medications as helping, then stay with what is working. Also, consult with the prescribing physician. A release form from the counselee may be necessary. Help him grow in competence while he is on medications. When he views the medications as no longer necessary, he may wish to slowly decrease the amounts—with medical supervision. Many will be able to do well without medication. But when it comes to medications, any action should be given thoughtful consideration. On no occasion should a counselee be encouraged to stop medication without medical consultation and supervision.

WHAT ABOUT PERSONALITY DISORDERS?

There are now believed to be eight different personality disorders. These designations may grow or some of them may be dismissed as new committees study them. I applaud this constant process of review and the readiness of the various study committees to make changes in designations when indicated. This reveals the DSM's true value—it describes observed emotional problems and gives practitioners a common language when discussing them. Yet it should not be viewed as an ordered presentation of physical diseases of the brain. For example, there is one less personality disorder in the DSM–4 than in the DSM–3R. Was this disease eradicated? Of course not—but the disorder, or label, was removed from the list.

Since it has not been established that these labels represent actual diseases, they must be treated as descriptive terms only. I have never had a counselee enter my office complaining of having a personality disorder unless he had picked up this label from previous counseling or from television.

One specific personality disorder is called a borderline personality disorder. This designation is an attempt to describe individuals who show a widespread pattern of unstable emotions, both within the person's image of himself and in his relationships. Moods fluctuate between intense anger and despair to feeling terrific. These moods are not specifically related to a crisis but more likely represent the individual's personality throughout his life up to this point. Granted, those with pervasive, lifelong emotional confusion are difficult to help—but not because of a disease. Rather, it is more likely a result of remaining, for a variety of personal and social reasons, in a *blaming position.*

One counselee, whom I will call Bill, came to me while I was serving as a chaplain at the Naval Station Brig in Norfolk, Virginia. Bill was professionally diagnosed as borderline by the Brig psychologist. His life revealed one crisis after another, with unstable personal relationships. Any support I offered him in counseling was manipulated into meeting his own immediate needs. I was continually asking him to consider his goal for coming to see me, even after numerous sessions.

Bill was able to conceptualize the difference between aspects of his life that revealed either a *willing position* or a *blaming position,* but he had been unable to incorporate these observations into his lifestyle. By the way, most professional counselors recognize a person described as borderline because of how frustrated the counselor becomes when trying to help him.

Bill claimed to be a Christian. I asked him during our sixth session what others would notice him doing differently when he is successfully living as a Christian. Not only could he not picture this, but he was unable to describe what a Christian was. This led to a discussion of the gospel message and his ultimate repentance and salvation. We prayed together that day, and he turned his life over to Christ. From that moment I chose to relate to him as a *new creation,* and I never let him forget it.

We now had a new foundation to build on and he learned to recognize a gradually clearer track leading to a potential for spiritual maturity. He could place himself on that track and visualize forward progress. As he began to achieve small successes, he experienced change that opened up a whole new world of order, patience, and personal responsibility. As you might imagine, my *supportive feedback* was filled with high fives!

Eventually Bill was released, and I counseled both him and his wife for a number of weeks. He is now active in a local church and moving forward with his wife in their life of faith. Although I spent more time with Bill than with most counselees I see, it was still brief in comparison to the length of time expected by secular therapists. According to one author, treatment of persons with borderline personality disorder may require as long as four to five years (Gunderson, 1988).

It is easier to help an individual return to the level of functioning he had before the onset of his problem or crisis than to assist one who cannot conceptualize emotional health at all. I doubt any other therapeutic approach would have been more helpful for Bill. But I believe a person who has *never known* emotional health first needs a new life in Christ. Could he deceive himself by imitating this belief of a new life in Christ? Certainly.

I try to keep in mind what Jesus said to the religious leaders of his day after they had said to Him, "If you are the Christ . . . tell us." His response was, "If I tell you, *you will not* believe me" (Luke 22:67 italics mine). The issue of the *will* remains crucial. Until a person is willing, he cannot truly enjoy a relationship with Christ, nor can he be helped through counseling.

WHAT OF PSYCHOTIC AND SCHIZOPHRENIC DISORDERS?

The standard treatment for psychotic disorders is the use of neuroleptic drugs. Neuroleptic means *attaching to the neuron.* Such drugs include major tranquilizers, antipsychotics, and neuroleptics. The term *neuroleptic* is now preferred for all three. Trade names include: Haldol, Thorazine, Stelazine, Vesprin, Mellaril, Prolixin, Navane, Trilafon, Tindal, Taractan, Loxitane, Moban, Serentil, Orap, Quide, Repoise, Compazine, and Dartal.

From five to ten million persons are using a neuroleptic at any time in America (Breggin, 1991, pp. 51–52). According to Breggin, who believes there is a need for reform in psychiatry, these medications represent a kind of chemical lobotomy. Lobotomy refers to the process of cutting the nerve connections between the frontal lobes of the brain and the rest of the brain. The frontal lobes generate the bulge in the human forehead—the feature that distinguishes us from animals. The frontal lobes represent the center of higher human functions: love, compassion, creativity, abstract reasoning, concern for others, the ability to visualize the future, initiative, willpower and determination, self-insight—all that is represented by being made in the image of God. Lobotomy destroys the frontal lobes, partially or permanently. Lobotomized patients are more accepting of a structured institutionalized setting, and this is why such operations were performed in state mental hospitals.

Neuroleptics impact the dopamine neurotransmitters, which provide the main pathways from the deeper brain to the frontal lobes. Just as surgery severs the nerve connections, neuroleptics interdict the nerve connections to the same region. These drugs produce a neurological lobotomy, basically a chemical lobotomy. Normal brain function is disabled. This was initially the primary purpose of neuroleptics, not merely a side effect.

Today the use of neuroleptics is more manageable and somewhat safer, but their benefit is of limited usefulness. This is not to imply that they have no benefit, only that their benefit is restricted. Obviously, they cannot produce abundant life. Indeed, they cannot produce a satisfying life. They can merely help maintain a life that would otherwise be severely out of control and tortured. But what are the patient's strengths, the exceptions to his emotional struggle? Do we address his areas of competence, or should we limit our assistance to medication?

I am reminded of the man who lived in the tombs, who could not be bound even with a chain. The Scripture says, "Night and day among the tombs and in the hills he would cry out and cut himself with stones. When he saw Jesus from a distance, he ran and fell on his knees in front of him. He shouted at the top of his voice, 'What do you want with me, Jesus, Son of the Most High God? Swear to God that you won't torture me!'" (Mark 5:5–7).

Jesus touched this man and restored him to health. When the villagers came to see what had happened, they "saw the man who had been possessed by the legion of demons, sitting there, dressed and in his right mind. . . ." (Mark 5:15). Jesus loved this man who was so tortured in his mind. His *intention* for him was not institutionalization nor a marginal existence. Rather, He lovingly restored him, preparing him for abundant life—demonstrating God's power.

I am aware that this incident may or may not represent a psychotic episode, but it is amazingly similar to it. I have no difficulty believing that if the text actually used this modern terminology, Jesus would still have rescued this man. It is so tempting to give up on such individuals even before we start.

I recall seeing one counselee who had been diagnosed as schizophrenic. I needed to remind myself of God's preparation for the counseling moment. The counselee was using Thorazine, among other medications, when I met him. He had been hearing voices, and his fear was that he would have to obey them. "Something bad is going to happen," he would say. He had been institutionalized earlier for three months. The Thorazine was helping him remain, for now, in an outpatient status.

It turned out that he had numerous exceptions and strengths that could be revealed as significant. He had never perceived himself to be the expert on his life, and he relished the idea when it was presented to him. We discussed how he had been able to manage up to this point. We also externalized the voices as a thought intrusion, and he proceeded to develop a clear description of what his life would be like without being manipulated by this intrusion, i.e., not having to obey such intruding thoughts.

During feedback we developed a one-day goal, and he was greatly motivated to take a greater measure of control back in his life. I saw him each day that week. He had new successes to report each day. I kept a close watch on him for weeks. He continues to make progress. Today he reports only occasional incidents in which he hears voices, and he tells of times when he deliberately begins to worship and praise God. He views each occasion as a test of his growing competence. His family is very supportive. He is doing well on his job and remains faithful in church. His doctor has greatly decreased his intake of Thorazine, and he may soon cease taking it altogether—while under supervision.

Should a church counselor treat persons with such complex problems? Yes and no. If he is not trained nor in consultation with a Christian psychiatrist, I would say no. With training and supervision, along with consultation, he should treat such a person—keeping in mind that this person may need greater attention for a longer period of time than many others whom he counsels. As always, adjunct support from family, friends, and the church is essential.

WHAT ABOUT DISSOCIATIVE IDENTITY DISORDERS?

Anyone who has been abused as a child needs special attention. There is evidence that children can separate or dissociate themselves from the abuse, developing alternate personalities in order to cope with the trauma. For example, a woman who is being traumatized through rape may tell herself that it is only her body that is being abused. In this way she separates herself from the unbearable trauma. But what if this abusive treatment happens to a child? What if the abuse continues for years? Such a child may develop alternate identities just to survive.

What used to be called multiple personality disorder is now more properly called a dissociative identity disorder. It does not represent a disease of the brain, such as Parkinsons, but rather a reaction of a frightened child who is desperately trying to survive. Whether or not the brain has been altered permanently is unknown.

As with the story of Carolyn, who had been sexually abused by her uncle, the goal is to encourage competence. The alternative is for the abused person to remain in the shadowland of victimhood. Even the drastic adaptation of dissociative identities is still a relative strength.

It is how this child coped. Yet the apostle Paul wrote, "When I was a child, I talked like a child, I thought like a child, I reasoned like a child. When I became a man, I put childish ways behind me" (1 Cor. 13:11).

So also, the world of the child must be incorporated into the life of the adult. Although this is a process that demands great patience, with a firm belief that change is inevitable, and as each alter ego is willing, an integration of personalities can be accomplished. It may be helpful to have the support of a counselor who has experience in working with dissociative identity disorders. Yet a person traumatized in this fashion primarily needs a persistent and patient counselor—one who is promoting personal competence, utilizing the counselee's strengths, and trusting in the intention of the Spirit of God.

Questions such as those dealt with above help to define the parameters of the SFPC approach. Keep in mind the purpose of this book is to aid the church counselor in becoming solution-focused. It is not an end but a beginning. Even during its writing, my thoughts have developed. A few of the case illustrations were individuals I was seeing during the months the book was being prepared and whose solutions found their way into the text. Also, as I reviewed the book I realized that some of my views had evolved after I started writing. This is to be expected. We are always changing, and this book is a reflection of that change in me. I look forward to receiving your suggestions and hearing about your experiences as well.

Throughout this book I have attempted to present a consistent theoretical design for becoming solution-focused in pastoral counseling. I have introduced specific tracks and procedures to equip the local church leaders for effective counseling. Counseling is cocreative and magnifies the strengths and competence of the counselee. The counselor is a detective looking for clues of God's preparation and sovereignty in the families, couples, and individuals who are seeking help.

Since SFPC is focused on outcome, it is usually brief. I can think of no reason to support long-term counseling when a shorter time in counseling will suffice. We do no disservice when our intention is to stay focused on solution and brevity. Indeed, in SFPC the motivation factor remains high and interest is maintained in therapeutic goals. Since the counselee is always changing, for better or for worse, I prefer to work for healthy change sooner rather than later. Yet it is essential to maintain the counseling relationship until the counselee agrees he is on track. Even then, occasional visits are recommended. If there is no church counselor, and the pastor does not have the time necessary for counseling—he should refer.

I maintain a firm belief that everyone needs a second chance. We need an opportunity to *start over*. Indeed, we need many such opportunities.

I remember an incident that happened when I was in the sixth grade. I was playing with matches in the boys' bathroom at school. My friend brought the matches, but I lit them. It was not enough that I lit one match; I lit the whole book at one time. Then, acting cool, but actually scared inside, I threw the lit matches into the trash container.

As I turned to leave, I thought I saw a flash of flame, but being immature, my friend and I simply left—as fast as possible. Unknown to us, another child saw the fire and immediately reported it to a teacher, thank God. Ten minutes later, the fire extinguished, this same child pointed me out to the school principal. "That's the boy," I heard him say. With these words, my heart sank, and I was doomed. With a firm grip on my ear, the principal removed me from the classroom.

The rest of that day was a blur. I knew I was in trouble, but I was not sure what lay before me. This was uncharted territory. I just wanted it all to go away. Perhaps, what I desperately needed was forgiveness. All I know is that in this instance, and in some others I have experienced during my life, I just wanted all the accusations and self-doubt to end. I desperately needed a fresh start.

I am still thankful for what actually happened. The town fire marshall came to my home to lecture me on fire safety, as my parents looked on, nodding their approval and respect. But I was never treated as deficient. No mention was ever made concerning an emotional disorder. No therapist suggested that I had an oppositional defiant disorder, or that perhaps I was ADD. No medications were recommended by an expert on such matters. These "disease" designations did not yet exist (although I certainly would have fit some of their criteria); therefore, I was not treated for them.

Instead, after being lectured by the principal, the fire department, and my parents, the matter was dropped. Life went on. No further mention was made of the incident in school or at home. I played with my friends, went to school, played baseball, and sometimes got into trouble. The birds continued to sing, the cool breeze continued to blow, and the world continued to turn. The sun came up in the morning just as it always had before. I was not labeled nor in any way treated as emotionally disturbed. I had my second chance to go on with life.

Grace offers not only *a* second chance, but seventy times seven chances. The person in emotional pain or confusion cries out for a fresh start. No counselee wants to be an interesting client or an interesting case for a therapist. Being labeled by an expert on mental disorders and hearing him use deficiency language often locks the counselee into his problems and disorientation. But as counselors we must remind ourselves that the counselee is a child of God, with his own dreams and hopes. He has only this one life. Indeed, the birds are singing, the sun is rising, the cool breeze is ready to caress his face. Jesus graciously won for him a fresh start. Counseling must offer this same opportunity. ▮

References

This list includes the publications to which the reader is referred throughout this volume and from which the author has drawn material.

Adams, J. E. (1970). *Competent to counsel.* Grand Rapids: Baker.

American Association of Pastoral Counselors (AAPC), 9508A Lee Hwy., Fairfax, VA 22031. Telephone: (703) 385–6967.

Bateson, G. (1980). *Mind and nature: A necessary unity.* New York: Ballantine.

Berg, I. K. (1990). *Solution-focused approach to family-based services.* Milwaukee: Brief Family Therapy Center.

Berg, I. K., & D. Gallagher. (1991). Solution-focused brief therapy with adolescent substance abusers. In T. C. Todd & M. D. Selekman (eds.), *Family therapy approaches with adolescent substance abusers* (93–111). Needham Heights, MA: Allyn & Bacon.

Berg, I. K., & S. D. Miller. (1992). *Working with the problem drinker: A solution-focused approach.* New York: W. W. Norton.

Breggin, P. R., M.D. (1991). *Toxic psychiatry.* New York: St. Martin's Press.

Brown, H. J., Jr., ed. (1991). *Live and learn and pass it on.* Nashville: Rutledge Hill.

Campbell, R. (1993). *How to really love your teenager.* Wheaton, IL: Victor Books.

Corey, G. (1991). *Theory and practice of counseling and psychotherapy.* Pacific Grove, CA: Brooks/Cole.

Crabb, L. (1988). *Inside out.* Colorado Springs: Navpress.

de Shazer, S. (1985). *Keys to solution in brief therapy.* New York: W. W. Norton.

de Shazer, S. (1988). *Clues: Investigating solutions in brief therapy.* New York: W. W. Norton.

de Shazer, S., & A. Molnar. (1984). Four useful interventions in brief family therapy. *Journal of Marital and Family Therapy,* 10 (3), 297–304.

Diagnostic and Statistical Manual of Mental Disorders, 4th ed. (1994) Washington, DC: American Psychiatric Association.

Durrant, M. (1993). *Creative strategies for school problems*. Epping, NSW, Australia: Eastwood Family Therapy Centre.

Durrant, M., & K. Kowalski. (1990). Overcoming the effects of sexual abuse: Developing a self-perception of competence. In M. Durrant & C. White (eds.), *Ideas for therapy with sexual abuse* (65–110). Adelaide: Dulwich Centre Publications.

Durrant, M. (1995). *After sexual abuse: Victimhood or competence?* Second Annual East Coast Solution-Focused Brief Therapy Conference. Epping NSW Australia: Eastwood Family Therapy Centre.

Erickson, M. H. (1954). Pseudo-orientation in time as a hypnotic procedure. *Journal of Clinical and Experimental Hypnosis*, 2, 161–283.

Furman, B., & T. Ahola. (1992). *Solution talk*. New York: W. W. Norton.

Glasser, W. (1976). *Reality therapy, a new approach to psychiatry.* New York: Harper & Row.

Glasser, W. (1984). *Take effective control of your life*. New York: Harper & Row.

Goolishian, H. (1991, October). *The dis-diseasing of mental health.* Plenary address presented at the Houston-Galveston Institute's Conference II, San Antonio, TX.

Gunderson, J. G. (1988). Personality disorders. In A. M. Nicholi, Jr. (ed.), *The new Harvard guide to psychiatry* (337–57). Cambridge, MA: Harvard University Press.

Huber, C., & B. Backlund. (1993). *The twenty-minute counselor.* New York: Continuum.

Kelly, G. (1955). *The psychology of personal constructs.* New York: W. W. Norton.

Kowalski, K., & R. Kral. (1989). The geometry of solution: Using the scaling technique, *Family Therapy Case Studies*, *4* (1), 59–66.

Lewis, C. S. (1942). *The screwtape letters*. London: Geoffrey Bles.

Lewis, C. S. (1944). *Screwtape proposes a toast and other pieces*, "Is Theology Poetry?" London: Collins-Fontana.

Lewis, C. S. (1946). *The great divorce.* New York: Macmillan.

Lewis, C. S. (1952). *Mere Christianity.* New York: Macmillan.

Lewis, C. S. (1953). *The silver chair.* New York: Macmillan.

Lewis, C. S. (1955). *Surprised by joy.* London: Geoffery Bles.

Lewis, C. S. (1961). *A grief observed.* London: Faber & Faber.

Lewis, C. S. (1966). *Letters of C. S. Lewis*. Edited by W. H. Lewis. London: Geoffrey Bles.

Lewis, C. S. (1967). *Letters to an American lady.* Edited by Clyde S. Kilby. Grand Rapids: Eerdmans.

Lewis, C. S. (1969). The vision of John Bunyan. *Selected literary essays.* Cambridge: Cambridge U P.

Lewis, C. S. (1970) *God in the dock.* Edited by Walter Hooper. Grand Rapids: Eerdmans.

Mercer, J. (1989). "Ac-cent-tchu-ate the positive. " *Your hit parade.* Time-Life Music, MCA Records.

Miller, S. (1995). *Common sense therapy: focusing on 'what works' in clinical practice.* Second Annual East Coast Solution-Focused Brief Therapy Conference. Chicago, IL.

O'Hanlon, W. H., & M. Weiner-Davis. (1989). *In search of solutions: A new direction in psychotherapy.* New York: W. W. Norton.

Powers, R. L., & J. Griffith. (1987). *Understanding life-style: The psycho-clarity process.* Chicago: American Instititute of Adlerian Studies.

Selekman, M. D. (1993). *Pathways to change.* New York: Guilford.

Seligman, L. (1990). *Selecting effective treatments.* San Francisco: Jossey-Bass.

Striano, J. (1987). *How to find a good psychotherapist: A consumer guide.* Santa Barbara, CA: Professional Press.

Tiggeman, J., & G. Smith. (1989). Adolescent 'shock therapy': Teenagers shocking their critics. *Dulwich Centre Newsletter* (Winter).

Walker, P. L. (1995). Integrity: Reality or illusion? *Advance* (Fall), 92. Springfield, MO: General Council of the Assemblies of God.

Walter, J. L., & E. Peller. (1992). *Becoming solution-focused in brief therapy.* New York: Brunner/Mazel.

Watzlawick, P., J. Weakland, & R. Fisch. (1974). *Change: Principles of problem formation and problem resolution.* New York: W. W. Norton.

White, M., & D. Epston. (1989). *Literate means to therapeutic ends.* Adelaide: Dulwich Centre Publications.

Subject Index

Name Index